Robert Moffat
The Missionary Hero of Kuruman

David J. Deane

Contents

Contents

ROBERT MOFFAT

THE MISSIONARY HERO

OF KURUMAN

BY

David J. Deane

ROBERT MOFFAT

The *Missionary Hero* of KURUMAN.

BY

DAVID J. DEANE,

AUTHOR OF "JOHN WICLIFFE, THE MORNING STAR OF THE REFORMA-
TION,"
"MARTIN LUTHER, THE REFORMER," ETC.

FIFTH EDITION. TWENTY-FIFTH THOUSAND.

FLEMING H. REVELL COMPANY

NEW YORK CHICAGO TORONTO

Publishers of Evangelical Literature.

[Illustration]

PREFACE

The record of a life like that of Robert Moffat, the South African missionary, can never be devoid of interest until all appreciation for noble deeds and patient endeavour becomes extinct in the heart of man. Till then, our pulses will quicken and our enthusiasm kindle as we read of dangers encountered and overcome, of the true courage that could undismayed encounter the king of beasts roaming on the African plain, and of passing the time with savage chiefs, beneath the spears and clubs of whose warriors thousands had been slain. Or our sympathy is awakened as stories of sickness and suffering, of hunger and terrible thirst, of trying disappointments, continued year after year, are related. Anon, gratitude causes the tear to start to our eye as we witness the love that prompts the effort to win the heathen to the Saviour, and see the once benighted ones clothed and subdued, learning in mind and heart the truth of the Gospel. Gratitude arises that we have men, heroic Christian men, who count nothing dear to them, not even their lives, that they may win sinners to the love of Jesus Christ.

Such an one was he, whose memoir we present to our readers, with the earnest desire that his strong faith may strengthen ours, that his quiet courage may excite us to perseverance in well-doing, and that his deliverance from manifold and very real dangers may lead us to place reliance upon Him in whom Moffat trusted, and who never forsakes those that trust in Him. May we all see, and especially the youth of our land, as we read the records of such noble lives, that true godliness detracts not from true manhood, but rather that it glorifies and ennobles it, until evil is overcome, and the wicked are put to silence.

In writing this brief sketch of the life of the Rev. Dr. Moffat, the author has been much indebted to those who have trodden the path before him; especially to the two well-known works, "Robert and Mary Moffat," by their son John S. Moffat, and to Robert Moffat's own book, "Missionary Labours and Scenes in South Africa." He also owes his acknowledgments to "The Missionary Magazine," "The Chronicle of the London Missionary Society," to the Reports of various Missionary Societies, "A Life's Labours in South Africa," and to other works from which information upon the subject has been gathered. To the two first named the author especially refers those of his readers who wish for fuller details than are given in this volume.

ROBERT MOFFAT.

CHAPTER I
PIONEER MISSIONS IN SOUTH AFRICA

The history of missions in South Africa abounds in interesting facts and incidents. Stories of heroism, strange adventures, and descriptions of journeyings among savage tribes and through countries frequented by beasts of prey, form part of its details. Its theme is love to God and love to man, and its facts have been called into existence through the efforts of noble-minded and true-hearted men and women to bring their coloured brethren and sisters to the knowledge of the Saviour, Jesus Christ.

Many names are held in veneration in connection with these missions, names of those who, having laboured faithfully upon earth, have been called to their reward; among these none stands forward with greater prominence than that of Robert Moffat.

A brief glance at the development of the colony at the Cape of Good Hope, and at the early efforts made to evangelise the native races, may enable the reader better to understand the work carried on by Robert Moffat, and the success achieved; also to realise something of the position of affairs when he first landed in South Africa.

Discovered by the Portuguese in 1486, it was not until the middle of the seventeenth century that much was done in the way of European colonisation. In 1652 the bold and mountainous promontory of the Cape was taken possession of by the Dutch, and a settlement was founded on the site of the present Cape Town. The earliest colonists were chiefly Dutch and German farmers; who were joined a little later on by numbers of French and Piedmontese Huguenots, driven from their native lands for conscience' sake.

At this early period the whole of what is now designated the Colony, was inhabited by Hottentots, a people lighter in colour than the Kafirs and Bechwanas, having pale yellow-brown skins, symmetrical in form when young, hardy, and having small hands and feet. They have nomadic tendencies; and, in their uncivilised state, scarcely practise agriculture. Their system of government is somewhat patriarchal; and they live in "kraals," or villages, consisting of bee-hive shaped huts, arranged in circular form. Their ideas of a Deity are extremely faint, they possess little in the nature of religious ceremonies, but the power of sorcerers among them is great. According to the locality occupied, they are known as Hottentots, Namaquas, or Corannas.

As the European colonists increased in numbers, they gradually advanced northward and eastward, either driving back the natives or subjugating them as slaves to their service. In 1806 the colony passed into the hands of the English, and, after a season of conflict, the Hottentots within the British territory were emancipated. This act of justice took place on 17th July, 1828.

In the early years of the present century, the natives of South Africa comprised—besides the Hottentots, who occupied the southern portion of the country, and were thinly scattered, to the north-west, in Great Namaqualand—the Kafirs, who dwelt in the south-east, beyond the Fish River; the Basutos, whose kraals were south of the Orange River; the Bechwanas and kindred tribes to the north of that river; and far away to the north-west, beyond Namaqualand, the Damara tribes, of whom but little was known at that time. Besides these, there were the Bushmen, a roving people, small in stature, and sunk to the lowest depths of barbarism, hunted down by the Dutch farmers like wild beasts, who had their hands turned against every man, and every man's hand turned against them.

To the Moravians belongs the honour of first seeking to bring the natives of South Africa under the influences of Christianity. In 1737 George Schmidt, who had been sent forth by the small Moravian church of Herrnhut, arrived in Cape Colony, and at Genadendal (the Vale of Grace), then known as Bavian's Kloof (the Glen of Baboons), established a mission station, where he laboured among the despised and oppressed Hottentots with much success for seven years. His work excited considerable opposition and persecution. He gathered a small Christian community and a school; but the Boers, or Dutch farmers, becoming jealous of the black population receiving education, he was summoned to Holland, and not allowed to return.

Fifty years elapsed before the Brethren were able to resume their work; but in 1792, three humble Christian artisans recommenced labour at Genadendal. The occupation of the colony by the British Government gave security to their mission, and it soon grew to be a large settlement, and a centre of light and civilisation to the surrounding country.

SOUTH AFRICA.

In 1799 the London Missionary Society commenced work in Cape Colony; at first by four brethren, who were shortly reinforced by Dr. J.P. Vanderkemp, a native of Holland, a man of rare gifts and dauntless courage. Successively scholar, cavalry officer, and physician, he was for some years a sceptic, but being converted through the drowning of his wife and child, and his own narrow escape from death, he commenced the earnest study of the Bible and the Eastern languages, and gained such wonderful proficiency in the latter, that it is stated he had a fair knowledge of sixteen.

Vanderkemp chose the Kafir tribes for his field of labour, and in 1799 proceeded from Graf Reinet, then the most distant colonial town, and that nearest to the Kafirs, to the headquarters of that people. Frequently in danger of his life, among those who considered the murder of a white man a meritorious deed, he worked and endured great hardship and privation, that he might make known the truths of the Gospel to the ignorant around, until the close of the year 1800, when, owing to a rebellion among the farmers, and the general unsettled state of the frontier, he was compelled to relinquish his mission.

Afterwards he laboured among the Hottentots of the colony with rare self-devotedness, often in great straits and many perils, but with frequent manifestations of the Divine blessing upon the work carried on. Finally, the Hottentot mission was transferred to Bethelsdorp, where steady progress was made. The scholars readily learned to read and write, and their facility in acquiring religious knowledge was astonishing, considering the peculiar apathy, stupidity, and aversion to any exertion, mental or corporeal, which characterised the natives. Dr. Vanderkemp died in 1811, after breathing out the Christian assurance, "All is well."

While Dr. Vanderkemp bent his steps towards Kafirland, three other missionaries, by name Kitcherer, Kramer, and Edwards, proceeded to the Zak River, between four hundred and five hundred miles north-east of Cape Town. Here a mission was established to the Bushmen, which, although unsuccessful in its original intention, became the finger-post to the Namaquas, Corannas, Griquas, and Bechwanas, for by means of that mission these tribes and their condition became known to the Christian world. After moving from their original location to the Orange River, at the invitation of a Griqua chief, Berend Berend by name, the mission was carried on among the Corannas, Namaquas, and Bastards (mixed races), finally removing in 1804 to Griqua Town, where it developed into the Griqua Mission, under Messrs. Anderson and Kramer, and became a powerful influence for good; continuing in existence for many years.

Mr. Anderson thus describes the condition of the Griquas when he first settled in their midst, and for some time afterwards:—

"They were without the smallest marks of civilisation. If I except one woman, they had not one thread of European clothing among them; and their wretched appearance and habits were such as might have excited in our minds an aversion to them, had we not been actuated by principles which led us to pity them, and served to strengthen us in pursuing the object of our missionary work; they were, in many instances, little above the brutes. It is a fact that we were present with them at the hazard of our lives. When we went among them they lived in the habit of plundering one another; and they saw no moral evil in this, nor in any of their actions. Violent deaths were common. Their usual manner of living was truly disgusting, and they were void of shame."

By missionary effort these unpromising materials yielded such fruit, that, in 1809, the congregation at Griqua Town consisted of 800 persons, who resided at or near the station during the whole or the greater part of the year. Besides their stated congregations the missionaries were surrounded by numerous hordes of Corannas and Bushmen, among whom they laboured. The land was brought under cultivation, and fields waving with corn and barley met the eye where all had been desolation and barrenness. In 1810 a threatened attack from a marauding horde of Kafirs was averted in answer to prayer. Mr. Janz, the only missionary then on the place, with the people, set apart a day for special supplication; they sent a pacific message and present to the Kafirs, who immediately retired. In place of war there was peace, and the blessings of civilisation followed the preaching of the Gospel.

A mission had also been commenced by the London Missionary Society in Great Namaqualand, north of the Orange River, on the western coast of Africa; a country of which the following description was given by an individual who had spent many years there: "Sir, you will find plenty of sand and stones, a thinly scattered population, always suffering from want of water, on plains and hills roasted like a burnt leaf, under the scorching rays of a cloudless sun."

The missionaries, after a journey of great difficulty and suffering, reached the land of the Namaquas, and halted for a time at a place which they named "Silent Hope," and then at "Happy Deliverance;" finally they settled at a spot, about one hundred miles westward of Africaner's kraal, called Warm Bath. Here, for a time, their prospects continued cheering. They were instant in season and out of season to advance the temporal and spiritual interests of the natives; though labouring in a debilitating climate; and in want of the common necessaries of life. Their congregation was increased by the desperado Jager, afterwards Christian Africaner, a Hottentot outlaw, who, with part of his people, occasionally attended to the instructions of the missionaries; and they visited the kraal of this robber chieftain in return. It was here that he first heard the Gospel, and, referring afterwards to his condition at this time, he said that he saw "men as trees walking."

Terrible trials soon came upon these devoted missionaries. Abraham Albrecht, one of their number died, and Africaner, becoming enraged, threatened an attack upon the station. The situation of the missionaries and their wives was most distressing. Among a feeble and timid people, with scarcely any means of defence, a bare country around, no mountain, glen, or cave in which they could take refuge, under a burning sun and on a glowing plain, distant two hundred miles from the abodes of civilised men, between which and them lay the dreary wilderness and the Orange River; such was their position, with the human lion in his lair, ready to rouse himself up to deeds of rapine and blood.

For a whole month they were in constant terror, hourly expecting the threatened attack. Their souls revolted at the idea of abandoning the people, who were suffering from want, to become a prey to a man from whom they could expect no quarter. On one occasion they dug a square hole in the ground, about six feet deep, that in case of an attack they might escape the musket balls. In this they remained for the space of a week, having the tilt sail of a waggon thrown over the mouth of the pit to keep off the burning rays of an almost vertical sun. Eventually they withdrew northward to the base of the Karas mountains, but finding it impossible to settle, retired to the Colony.

Africaner approached the station, and finding it deserted, plundered it of whatever articles could be found; one of his followers afterwards setting fire to the houses and huts. Thus for a season, this mission was brought to a close. It was after a time resumed at a place south of the Orange River named Pella.

Thus missions in South Africa had been commenced, stations among the Hottentots and others had been formed, good work had been done, and the way pioneered. The field was opened and it was wide, but as yet the labourers were few.

At the time when Vanderkemp closed his eyes on this world, a lad was working as an apprentice to a Scotch gardener, rising in the dense darkness of the cold winter's mornings at four o'clock, and warming his knuckles by knocking them against the handle of his spade. He was passing through a hard training, but this lad was being prepared to take up the work which Vanderkemp had so well begun, though in a somewhat different sphere, and to repair the loss which had been sustained by the missionary cause through his death. The name of this lad was Robert Moffat.

CHAPTER II
CHILDHOOD AND YOUTH

Robert Moffat was born on the 21st of December, 1795. His parents dwelt at that time at Ormiston, in East Lothian, Scotland. They were pious God-fearing people; the mother though holding a stern religious faith, yet possessed a most tender loving heart, and very early sought to instil into the minds and hearts of her children the love of God and a knowledge of the Holy Scriptures.

Of the early childhood of the future missionary very little is stated. In 1797 his father received an appointment in the Custom House at Portsoy, and in 1806 the home of the Moffats was at Carronshore, on the Firth of Forth. At this time the family consisted of four sons and two daughters, besides the subject of this memoir.

A glimpse of the interior of their cottage, during the long winter evenings, is given, which shows how the mother by her gentle influence may become the means of sowing seed, which shall spring up in after years bearing fruit a hundred-fold. The lads were gathered by the fireside learning to knit and sew, and while so engaged their mother, who took great interest in the missionary enterprises then carried on, read aloud, in such publications as she could obtain, the descriptions given of the work and sufferings of the pioneer labourers in heathen lands, more especially of the Moravians in Greenland and the East Indies.

Of educational advantages, Robert had but few in his early days. One, "Wully Mitchell," as he was popularly called, the parish schoolmaster was his first tutor; and "the Shorter Catechism," the title-page of which contained the alphabet, his first instruction book. His progress was but slow, his hands often being made to suffer for the dullness of his brains. A boy living in the midst of shipping, his desires were more for nautical matters than for Wully's books, and so he ran off to sea. The captain of the ship on which he was, became much attached to the lad, so with his parent's consent, he made several voyages in the coasting trade. Many hairbreadth escapes fell to his lot, and at last he quitted the sea, as he states "to the no small joy of my parents."

When about eleven he accompanied his elder brother, Alexander, to Mr. Paton's school at Falkirk. This school was for writing and book-keeping, but such as chose to pay received lessons in astronomy and geography after school hours. Alexander was one of these, and Robert was allowed to wait for his brother in the large room while the class was being conducted. "I felt queer," he tells us "to know what the master was doing within the circle, and used to look very attentively through any little slip of an opening under an elbow, while I eagerly listened to the illustrations given, the master all the while never suspecting that I was capable of understanding the planetary system. What I could not understand my brother explained on our way home." In this manner he picked up some knowledge of astronomy.

At this school the lad continued for six months. It was the last he ever attended.

When about fourteen, Robert Moffat was apprenticed to a gardener, named John Robertson, a just but hard man, who lived at Parkhill, Polmont. The toil was severe and the food scanty. Often in the bitter cold of a Scottish winter the lads employed were required to commence work at four o'clock in the morning, and had to hammer their knuckles against the handles of their spades to try and bring some feeling into them. Here he remained till the end of 1812.

While thus engaged, he managed to attend an evening class occasionally, and made an attempt at learning Latin and mensuration. He also picked up some knowledge of the smith's craft, and acquired sufficient skill to play a little on the violin. A special craving, which stood him in good stead in after life, impelled him to learn something of whatever he came in contact with.

Upon the completion of his apprenticeship, in 1812, he obtained a situation at Donibristle, a seat of the Earl of Moray at Aberdour. Here, he delighted his fellow-workers of an evening by his violin performances, was fond of athletic sports, in which he excelled, and became an accomplished swimmer, saving the life of one of his companions, who having got out of his depth was in imminent danger of drowning.

In this situation he continued about a twelvemonth, and then, being about sixteen, he found employment as under-gardener to Mr. Leigh, of High Leigh, in Cheshire. While at Donibristle he had been able to frequently visit his parents; the time had now come when he must bid them adieu.

The parting scene between Robert and his mother has been sketched by his own hand and appeared in the Bible Society's "Gleanings for the Young." It is described as follows:—

"When we came within sight of the spot where we were to part, perhaps never again to meet in this world, she said—

"'Now, my Robert, let us stand here for a few minutes, for I wish to ask one favour of you before we part, and I know you will not refuse to do what your mother asks.'

"'What is it, mother?' I inquired.

"'Do promise me first that you will do what I am now going to ask, and I shall tell you.'

"'No, mother, I cannot till you tell me what your wish is.'

"'O Robert, can you think for a moment that I shall ask you, my son, to do anything that is not right? Do not I love you?'

"'Yes, mother, I know you do; but I do not like to make promises which I may not be able to fulfil.'

"I kept my eyes fixed on the ground. I was silent, trying to resist the rising emotion. She sighed deeply. I lifted my eyes and saw the big tears rolling down the cheeks which were wont to press mine. I was conquered, and as soon as I could recover speech, I said—

"'O mother! ask what you will and I shall do it.'

"'I only ask you whether you will read a chapter in the Bible every morning and another every evening?'

"I interrupted by saying, 'Mother, you know I read my Bible.'

"'I know you do, but you do not read it regularly, or as a duty you owe to God, its Author.' And she added: 'Now I shall return home with a happy heart, inasmuch as you have promised to read the Scriptures daily. O Robert, my son, read much in the New Testament. Read much in the Gospels—the blessed Gospels; then you cannot well go astray. If you pray, the Lord Himself will teach you.'

"I parted from my beloved mother, now long gone to that mansion about which she loved to speak. I went on my way, and ere long found myself among strangers. My charge was an important one for a youth, and though possessing a muscular frame and a mind full of energy, it required all to keep pace with the duty which devolved upon me. I lived at a considerable distance from what are called the means of grace, and the Sabbaths were not always at my command. I met with none who appeared to make religion their chief concern. I mingled, when opportunities offered, with the gay and godless in what are considered innocent amusements, where I soon became a favourite; *but I never forgot my promise to my mother*."

After several delays, High Leigh was reached on Saturday, 26th December, 1813, and there the young man found himself surrounded by a genial atmosphere. The head gardener took to him, and soon left a great deal in his hands. This made his work very heavy and responsible; but, although labouring almost day and night, he yet managed to devote some time to the study of such books as he could obtain. The kindly notice of Mrs. Leigh was attracted to him, and she lent him books, and encouraged him to studious pursuits.

In very early years serious impressions had been made upon the heart of Robert Moffat. The earnest teachings of his minister, combined with his mother's counsels and prayers, left recollections which could never be effaced. These impressions were now to be deepened, and the good seed that had been sown to be quickened. The Wesleyan Methodists had commenced a good work at High Leigh, and a pious Methodist and his wife induced Moffat to attend some of their meetings. He became convinced of his state as a sinner, and unhappy, but after a severe and protracted struggle, he found pardon, justification, and peace, through faith in Jesus Christ, and henceforth his life was devoted to the service of his Lord. Energetically he threw himself into the society and work of his new friends, but by so doing, lost the goodwill of Mr. and Mrs. Leigh, who were grieved that one in whom they took so much interest should have become a Methodist. So were these good people despised by many in those days.

At this time Robert's worldly prospects were brightening, and a position of honour and comfort seemed opening before him. But the anticipations of that day were not to be.

Apparently unimportant events frequently determine the whole course of our lives, and a simple incident was now about to change the current of this young man's life, and to convert the rising gardener into the God-honoured and much-beloved missionary. How this came to pass we now relate:

While at High Leigh, Robert Moffat had occasion to visit Warrington, a town about six miles distant He set off one calm summer evening. All nature seemed at rest, and thoughts of God and a feeling of admiration for His handiworks took possession of the young man's mind. His life was reviewed, and with thoughts full of hope he entered the town. Passing over a bridge he noticed a placard. It contained the announcement of a missionary meeting, over which the Rev. William Roby, of Manchester, was to preside. He had never seen such an announcement before. He read the placard over and over again, and, as he did so, the stories told by his mother of the Moravian missionaries in Greenland and Labrador, which had been forgotten for years, came vividly to mind. From that moment, his choice was made; earthly prospects vanished: his one thought was, "how to become a missionary?"

Many difficulties seemed to stand in the way between Robert and the accomplishment of his desire, but the same Divine power which had implanted the desire, prepared the way for its fulfilment. He visited Manchester, shortly after the event just related, to be present at a Wesleyan Conference; and while there, with much hesitancy and trepidation, ventured to knock at the door of Mr. Roby's house and request an interview with that gentleman. He was shown into the parlour, and the man whom he had been hoping, yet dreaded, to see, quickly made his appearance. "He received me with great kindness," said Moffat, "listened to my simple tale, took me by the hand, and told me to be of good courage."

The result of this interview was a promise on Mr. Roby's part to write to the Directors of the London Missionary Society concerning him, and to communicate their wishes to him as soon as they were received. In the meantime Robert returned to his ordinary occupation.

After waiting a few weeks a summons came from Mr. Roby for Moffat to visit Manchester again; and, with the view of his studying under the care and instruction of that reverend gentleman, it was arranged that he should accept a situation in a nursery garden belonging to Mr. Smith, at Dukinfield, that place being near at hand. Moffat continued here about a year, visiting Mr. Roby once or twice each week. Mr. and Mrs. Smith were a pious and worthy couple, and their house was a house of call for ministers. They were always ready for every good work whether at home or abroad.

"In all thy ways acknowledge Him, and He shall direct thy paths," is one of the maxims of Holy Writ that should be engraven upon the heart and mind of every youth and maiden. Robert Moffat's desire was for the glory of God and the extension of the Redeemer's kingdom, and God was not only opening the way for His servant, but was preparing a faithful and devoted helpmate for him in his various spheres of labour through life.

Robert's employer had an only daughter, named Mary, beautiful of countenance, but more beautiful in heart. She had been educated at the Moravian school at Fairfield, and was distinguished for fervent piety and deep sympathy with the missionary cause. The two young folks were thrown together, mutual esteem deepened into love, and the maiden, possessed with so large a missionary spirit, was prepared to share the lot of the young herald of the Cross. For a time, however, it was ordained that Robert should pursue his course alone.

After being at Dukinfield nearly a year, the Directors resolved to accept the services of Robert Moffat. He left Mr. Smith's employment and removed to Manchester, so that he might be close to Mr. Roby, to receive such superintendence as was possible in his studies. This period extended to but a few months, so that of college training and opportunities Robert had little experience.

The time rapidly drew near for his departure abroad. A hurried visit was paid to the parents whom he never expected to see again, and then he awaited his call to the mission field.

On the 13th of September, 1816, after bidding farewell to Mr. Roby, whose "kindness, like that of a father," wrote Moffat, "will not be easily obliterated from my mind," he started for London. While in the Metropolis he visited the Museum at the Rooms of the London Missionary Society, and the following extract from a letter to his parents, in connection with this visit, shows the spirit which actuated the youthful missionary at this time:—

"I spent some time in viewing the Museum, which contains a great number of curiosities from China, Africa, the South Seas, and the West Indies. It would be foolish for me to give you a description. Suffice it to say that the sight is truly awful, the appearance of the wild beasts is very terrific, but I am unable to describe the sensations of my mind when gazing on the objects of Pagan worship. Alas! how fallen are my fellow-creatures, bowing down to forms enough to frighten a Roman soldier, enough to shake the hardest heart. Oh that I had a thousand lives, and a thousand bodies; all of them should be devoted to no other employment but to preach Christ to these degraded, despised, yet beloved mortals."

With such enthusiasm he prepared to enter upon the work that lay before him.

CHAPTER III
DEPARTURE FOR THE CAPE

The valedictory service was held at Surrey Chapel on the 30th of September. Nine missionaries were set apart; four for the South Seas, one of whom was John Williams, the martyr of Erromanga, and five for South Africa. At first it had been intended that Robert Moffat should accompany John Williams, but this was subsequently altered.

The missionaries for Africa embarked at Gravesend on the 18th of October in the *Alacrity*, and after a prosperous voyage reached Cape Town on the 13th of January, 1817.

Two of the party were appointed to stations within the colony; Moffat and Kitchingman were destined for Namaqualand. Before they could proceed on their journey, however, permission had to be obtained from the Government, and this was at first refused.

While detained in the colony, Moffat lodged with a Dutch farmer, at a village thirty-six miles from Cape Town, named Stellenbosch. Here he learnt Dutch, an acquisition of great advantage to him in after life, as it enabled him to preach to the Boers, and to as many of their native servants as understood that language. He also accompanied the Rev. George Thorn, of the Dutch Reformed Church, on an evangelistic tour. It occupied six weeks, during which time they rode a distance of about seven hundred miles.

After a further sojourn at Stellenbosch, Moffat visited Cape Town, and busied himself in gaining such practical knowledge as came within his reach. He also visited the military hospital there. Many of the soldiers were Scotch, and he had a warm heart for soldiers, his brother Alexander having gone to India in the ranks some years before.

At last the requisite permission came, and Moffat and Kitchingman prepared for their journey. Waggons were bought, oxen hired, leave taken of friends, and on the 22nd of September, 1817, Mr. and Mrs. Kitchingman, Robert Moffat, and a missionary named Ebner, who, for a time, had been with Africaner, and who had come to Cape Town for supplies, set out on their way to Namaqualand.

The history of the Namaqualand Mission has been sketched in outline in our introductory chapter. Africaner, although an outlaw and a terror to the farmers of the colony, had a respect for the English. He visited the missionaries on one occasion, prior to their removal to Warm Bath, and said, "I love the English, for I have always heard that they are the friends of the poor black man." He also sent his children to them for instruction; yet subsequent events, as we have seen, enraged him, and led him to destroy the mission station at Warm Bath.

The Rev. J. Campbell, in his first visit to Africa, 1812-1814, crossed the interior of the continent to Namaqualand. During his journey, he found in every village through which he passed the terror of Africaner's name; and he afterwards said "that he and his retinue never were so afraid in their lives." From Pella, where the mission station then was, Mr. Campbell wrote a conciliatory letter to Africaner, in consequence of which that chieftain agreed to receive a missionary at his kraal. Mr. Ebner had been sent from Pella, and had been labouring for a short time previous to his visit to the Cape in 1817. Good had been accomplished, Africaner and his two brothers, David and Jacobus, had been baptised, but then the situation of the missionary became extremely trying, he lost influence with the people, and his property, and even his life, were in danger.

Soon after leaving Cape Town, Mr. Ebner parted company with the Kitchingmans and Moffat, and they pursued their way alone. The details of the journey illustrate the difficulties of travelling in South Africa in those days. "In perils oft," aptly expresses the condition of the missionary in his wanderings, as he travelled mile after mile, often over dreary wastes of burning sand, famished with hunger, parched with thirst, with the howl of the hyena and the roar of the lion disturbing his slumbers at night, and with Bushmen, more savage than either, hovering near, ever ready to attack the weak and defenceless.

The farmers, from whom the travellers received hospitality as they passed the boundaries of the colony, were very sceptical as to the conversion of Africaner, and gloomy indeed were their predictions as to the fate of the youthful missionary now venturing into the power of the outlaw chief. One said Africaner would set him up for his boys to shoot at, another that he would strip off his skin to make a drum with, and a third predicted he would make a drinking-cup of his skull. A kind motherly dame said, as she wiped the tear from her eye and bade him farewell, "Had you been an old man it would have been nothing, for you would soon have died, whether or no; but you are young, and going to become a prey to that monster."

On one occasion Moffat halted at a farm belonging to a Boer, a man of wealth and importance, who had many slaves. Hearing that he was a missionary, the farmer gave him a hearty welcome, and proposed in the evening that he should give them a service. To this he readily assented, and supper being ended, a clearance was made, the big Bible and the psalm-books were brought out, and the family was seated. Moffat inquired for the servants, "May none of your servants come in?" said he.

"Servants! what do you mean?"

"I mean the Hottentots, of whom I see so many on your farm."

"Hottentots!" roared the man, "are you come to preach to Hottentots? Go to the mountains and preach to the baboons; or, if you like, I'll fetch my dogs, and you may preach to them."

The missionary said no more but commenced the service. He had intended to challenge the "neglect of so great salvation," but with ready wit seizing upon the theme suggested by his rough entertainer, he read the story of the Syrophenician woman, and took for his text the words, "Truth, Lord, yet the dogs eat of the crumbs which fall from their masters' table." He had not proceeded far in his discourse when the farmer stopped him, saying, "Will Mynherr sit down and wait a little, he shall have the Hottentots."

He was as good as his word, the barn was crowded, the sermon was preached, and the astonished Hottentots dispersed. "Who," said the farmer, "hardened your hammer to deal my head such a blow? I'll never object to the preaching of the Gospel to Hottentots again."

After a toilsome march, during which Mr. Kitchingman and Moffat took it in turn to drive the cattle, losing some through the hyenas by the way, they reached Bysondermeid, to which station Mr. and Mrs. Kitchingman had been appointed. There Robert stayed one month, receiving much useful information from Mr.

Schmelen, the missionary whom Mr. Kitchingman had come to replace, he having been ordered to Great Namaqualand, where he had laboured before.

At length, his oxen being rested, Robert Moffat bade adieu to Mr. and Mrs. Kitchingman, whose friendship he much valued, and with a guide and drivers for the oxen started onward. Their way led through a comparatively trackless desert, and they travelled nearly the whole night through deep sand. Those were not the days of railway trains, and travelling had to be undertaken in cumbrous, springless bullock-waggons, several spare oxen being taken to provide for losses and casualties. Towards morning the oxen were so exhausted that they began to lie down in the yoke from fatigue, compelling a halt before water had been reached. The journey was resumed the next day, but still no water could be found.

As it appeared probable that if they continued in the same direction, they would perish through thirst, they altered their course to the northward, but the experiences were as bad as before. At night they lay down exhausted and suffering extremely from thirst, and the next morning rose at an early hour to find the oxen incapable of moving the waggon a step farther. Taking them and a spade to a neighbouring mountain, a large hole was dug in the sand, and at last a scanty supply of water was obtained. This resembled the old bilge-water of a ship for foulness, but both men and oxen drank of it with avidity.

In the evening, when about to yoke the oxen to the waggon, it was found that most of them had run off towards Bysondermeid. No time was to be lost, so Moffat instantly sent off the remaining oxen with two men to solicit assistance from Mr. Bartlett at Pella, while he remained behind with his goods. "Three days," said he afterwards, "I remained with my waggon-driver on this burning plain, with scarcely a breath of wind, and what there was felt as if coming from the mouth of an oven. We had only tufts of dry grass to make a small fire or rather flame; and little was needed as we had scarcely any food to prepare. We saw no human being, not a single antelope or beast of prey made its appearance, but in the dead of night we sometimes heard the roar of the lion on the mountain. At last when we were beginning to fear that the men had either perished or wandered, Mr. Bartlett arrived on horseback, with two men having a quantity of mutton tied to their saddles. I cannot conceive of an epicure gazing on a table groaning under the weight of viands, with half the delight that I did on the mutton."

WAGGON TRAVELLING IN SOUTH AFRICA.

Fresh oxen, accustomed to deep sand, conveyed the weary travellers to Pella, where Moffat remained a few days, being greatly invigorated in mind and body by the Christian kindness of Mr. and Mrs. Bartlett and the friendly attentions of the heathen converts.

Starting again, he came to the Orange River, crossing which was generally a work of difficulty at that time. The native teacher from Warm Bath, who had come to Pella to conduct Moffat to his village, led the missionary to a ford opposite to that place. The waggon and its contents were swam over on a fragile raft of dry willow logs—a laborious and tedious operation, the raft having to be taken to pieces after each journey, and the separate logs conveyed back again by swimmers. All the goods being over, Robert was asked to place himself upon the raft. Not altogether liking its appearance, and also wishing to save the natives trouble, he took off his clothes and, leaving them to be conveyed across, plunged into the stream. The natives were afraid as they saw him approach the middle of the current, and some of their most expert swimmers sprang in to overtake him, but in vain. When he emerged on the northern bank, one of them came up out of breath and said, "Were you born in the great sea water?"

Robert Moffat reached Africaner's kraal on the 26th of January, 1818, and was kindly received by Mr. Ebner. The chief soon made his appearance, and inquired if the new missionary had been appointed by the Directors in London. Receiving an affirmative reply, he ordered a number of women to come. Then pointing to a spot of ground he said to the women, "There you must build a house for the missionary." In half an hour the structure was completed, in appearance something like a bee-hive. In this frail house, of sticks and native mats, Moffat lived for nearly six months, being scorched by the sun, drenched by the rain, exposed to the wind, and obliged often to decamp through the clouds of dust; in addition to which, any dog wishing for a night's lodging could force its way through the wall, sometimes to the loss of the missionary's dinner next day. A serpent was occasionally found coiled in a corner, or the indweller of the habitation had to spring up, in the middle of the night, to save himself and his house from being crushed to pieces during the nocturnal affrays of the cattle which roamed at large. He lived principally upon milk and dried meat, until, after a time, he was able to raise a little grain and garden stuff.

A few days after Moffat's arrival, Mr. Ebner departed, so that the young missionary was left entirely alone in a trying and most difficult position, a stranger in the midst of a strange people. "Here I was," said he, "left alone with a people suspicious in the extreme; jealous of their rights which they had obtained at the point of the sword; and the best of whom Mr. Ebner described as a sharp thorn. I had no friend and brother with whom I could participate in the communion of saints, none to whom I could look for counsel or advice. A barren and miserable country; a small salary, about twenty-five pounds per annum. No grain, and consequently no bread, and no prospect of getting any, from the want of water to cultivate the ground, and destitute of the means of sending to the Colony. These circumstances led to great searchings of heart, to see if I had hitherto aimed at doing and suffering the will of Him in whose service I had embarked. Satisfied that I had not run unsent, and having in the intricate, and sometimes obscure course I had come, heard the still small voice saying, 'This is the way, walk ye in it,' I was wont to pour out my soul among the granite rocks surrounding this station, now in sorrow, and then in joy; and more than once I have taken my violin, once belonging to Christian Albrecht, and, reclining upon one of the huge masses, have, in the stillness of the evening, played and sung the well-known hymn, a favourite of my mother's—

> 'Awake, my soul, in joyful lays,
> To sing the great Redeemer's praise.'"

Robert Moffat looked to his God for help and guidance, and his heart was strengthened.

At this period the chief, Christian Africaner, was in a doubtful state of mind; while Titus, his brother, a man of almost reckless courage, was a fearful example of ungodliness, and a terror to most of the inhabitants on the station. Soon after the commencement of his stated services—which were, according to the custom of the missionaries at that period, religious service morning and evening, and school for three or four hours during the day—the heart of the youthful missionary was much cheered by noticing the regular attendance of the chief. Although not a fluent reader, the New Testament became his constant companion, and a change passed over him apparent to all. The lion at whose name many trembled became a lamb, and the love of Jesus Christ filled his heart. He who was formerly like a fire-brand, spreading discord, enmity, and war among the neighbouring tribes, was now ready to make any sacrifice to avoid conflict, and besought parties at variance with each other to be at peace.

Even Titus was subdued, and although he never made a profession, yet he became a steady and unwavering friend to the missionary, and many times ministered to his wants. "I hear what you say," he would reply when the truth was pressed upon him, "and I think I sometimes understand, but my heart will not feel." Two other brothers of the chief, David and Jacobus, became believers and zealous assistants in the work of the mission.

The extreme heat endured in the native house, and the character of the food, milk and meat only, brought on a severe attack of bilious fever, which in the course of two days induced delirium. Opening his eyes as soon as consciousness returned, Moffat saw his attendant and Africaner sitting beside his couch, gazing upon him with eyes full of sympathy and tenderness. Taking some calomel he speedily recovered, and was soon at his post again.

The place where Africaner dwelt being quite unsuitable for a permanent mission-station, on account of the scarcity of water, it was determined to take a journey northward to examine a country on the border of Damaraland, where it was reported that fountains of water abounded. There was, however, only one waggon and that a cripple, and neither carpenters nor smiths were at the station to repair it. Without it they could not go, so after thinking the matter over Moffat undertook its repair. Before doing so he must needs have a forge, and a forge meant bellows; but here was a difficulty, the native bellows were of no use for the work in hand. He therefore contrived, by means of two goat-skins and a circular piece of board, to make a pair of bellows of sufficient power to fan the fire and heat the iron, and with a blue granite stone for an anvil, a pair of tongs indicative of Vulcan's first efforts, and a hammer, never intended for its present use, he successfully accomplished his task, and afterwards repaired some gun-locks, which were as essential for the comfort and success of the journey as the waggon.

The party that set out was a large one, including Africaner, three of his brothers, and Moffat. The country which they passed through was sterile in the extreme, and the expedition proved a failure. They therefore returned home again after an absence of a few weeks. The school and mission services were resumed, but, as David and Jacobus Africaner were now able assistants, Moffat undertook itinerating visits on a more extensive scale than he had done before. For this purpose Titus presented him with his only horse. Previously Moffat had ridden upon a bullock with horns, a dangerous practice, as, if the bullock stumbles, the rider may be thrown forward and transfixed upon them.

Privations and dangers frequently attended these itinerating journeys. Referring to one of them Robert Moffat states, "After tying my Bible and hymn-book in a blanket to the back of my saddle, and taking a good draught of milk, I started with my interpreter, who rode upon an ox. We had our guns, but nothing in our purse or scrip, save a pipe, some tobacco, and a tinder-box. After a hot day's ride to reach a village, the people would give us a draught of sweet milk, and then old and young, assembling in a nook of the fold, among the kine, would listen to my address on the great concerns of their soul's salvation. I exhorted those who could read to read to others and try to teach them to do the same, promising them a reward in heaven, for I had none to give on earth. When service was over, having taken another draught of milk, and renewed my conversation with the people, I lay down on a mat to repose for the night. Sometimes a kind housewife would hang a bamboos, a wooden vessel filled with milk, on a forked stick near my head, that I might, if necessary, drink during the night."

Once he slept on the ground near the hut in which the principal man of the village and his wife reposed. During the night a noise as of cattle broken loose was heard. In the morning he remarked upon this to his host, when that individual replied, "Oh, I was looking at the spoor this morning, it was the lion!" adding that a few nights previously a goat had been seized from the very spot on which Moffat had been sleeping. Upon Moffat asking him why he had put him to sleep there, the man replied, "Oh, the lion would not have the audacity to jump over on you."

Sometimes it happened that after travelling all day, hoping to reach a village at night, the travellers would find when they got to the place that all the people had gone. Then hungry and thirsty they had to pass the night. In the morning after searching for water, and partaking of a draught if they were successful in finding it, they would start off again with their hunger unsatisfied, and deem themselves fortunate if they overtook the migrating party that evening.

Of his ordinary manner of living at this time, he says, "My food was milk and meat, living for weeks together on one, and then for a while on the other, and again on both together. All was well so long as I had either, but sometimes they both failed, and there were no shops in the country where I could have purchased, and, had there been any, I must have bought on credit, for money I had none."

His wardrobe bore the same impress of poverty as his larder. The clothes received when in London soon went to pieces, and the knowledge of sewing and knitting, unwillingly learnt from his mother, often now stood him in good stead. She once showed him how a shirt might be smoothed by folding it properly and hammering it with a piece of wood. Resolving one day to have a nice one for the Sabbath, Moffat tried this plan. He folded the shirt carefully, laid it on a smooth block of stone—not a hearth-stone, but a block of fine granite—and hammered away. "What are you doing?" said Africaner. "Smoothing my shirt," replied his white friend. "That is one way," said he, and so it was, for on holding the shirt up to the light it was seen to be riddled with holes. "When I left the country," said Moffat,

"I had not half-a-dozen shirts with two sleeves apiece."

Robert Moffat's stay in Namaqualand extended to a little over twelve months. Near its close he made on Africaner's account—with the view of ascertaining the suitability of a place for settlement—a journey to the Griqua country, and after a terrible experience, in which he suffered from hunger, thirst, heat, and drinking poisoned water, he reached Griqua Town, and entered the house of Mr. Anderson, the missionary there, speechless, haggard, emaciated, and covered with perspiration, making the inmates understand by signs that he needed water. Here he was most kindly entertained, and after a few days started back again. The return journey was almost as trying as the outward one, but he reached Vreede Berg (Africaner's village) in safety. The chief received Moffat's account of his researches with entire satisfaction, but the removal of himself and people was allowed to remain prospective for a season.

Missionary labours were resumed. The school flourished, and the attendance at the Sabbath services was most encouraging. The people were so strongly attached to their missionary, that although he was contemplating a visit to the Cape, he dared not mention the subject to them. In a letter written at this time, alluding to his every-day life, he says, "I have many difficulties to encounter, being alone. No one can do anything for me in my household affairs. I must attend to everything, which often confuses me, and, indeed, hinders me in my work, for I could wish to have almost nothing to do but to instruct the heathen, both spiritually and temporally. Daily I do a little in the garden, daily I am doing something for the people in mending guns. I am carpenter, smith, cooper, shoemaker, miller, baker, and housekeeper—the last is the most burdensome of any. An old Namaqua woman milks my cows, makes a fire, and washes. All other things I do myself, though I seldom prepare anything till impelled by hunger. I drink plenty of milk, and often eat a piece of dry meat. Lately I reaped nearly two bolls of wheat from two hatfuls which I sowed. This is of great help to me. I shall soon have plenty of Indian corn, cabbages, melons, and potatoes. Water is scarce. I have sown wheat a second time on trial. I live chiefly now on bread and milk. To-day I churned about three Scotch pints of milk, from which there were two pounds of butter, so you may conceive that the milk is rich. I wish many times that my mother saw me. My house is always clean, but oh what a confusion there is among my linen."

In November, 1818, letters reached Robert Moffat from England. One came from Miss Smith, in which that young lady stated that she had most reluctantly renounced hope of ever getting abroad, her father determining never to allow her to do so. This was a sore trial, but it only led the child closer to his Father, and that Father, who doeth all things well, in His own good time, brought to pass that which now seemed impossible.

Early in 1819, circumstances required Mr. Moffat to visit Cape Town. Conversing with Africaner on the state and prospects of missions, the idea flashed into Moffat's mind that it would be well for that chief to accompany him, and he suggested it to his coloured friend. Africaner was astonished. "I had thought you loved me," said he, "and do you advise me to go to the Government to be hung up as a spectacle of public justice?"

AFRICANER.

Then, putting his hand to his head, he said, "Do you not know that I am an outlaw, and that one thousand rix-dollars have been offered for this poor head?" After a little while he replied to the missionary's arguments by saying, "I shall deliberate and *roll* (using the words of the Dutch Version of the Bible) my way upon the Lord. I know He will not leave me."

To get Africaner safely through the territories of the Dutch farmers to the Cape was a hazardous proceeding, as the atrocities he had committed were not forgotten, and hatred against him still rankled in many a breast. However, attired in one of the only two substantial shirts Moffat had left, a pair of leather trousers, a duffel jacket, much the worse for wear, and an old hat, neither white nor black, the attempt was made, the chief passing as one of the missionary's attendants. His master's costume was scarcely more refined than his own.

As a whole, the Dutch farmers were kind and hospitable to strangers, and as Moffat reached their farms, some of them congratulated him on returning alive, they having been assured that Africaner had long since murdered him. At one farm a novel and amusing instance occurred of the state of feeling concerning them both. As they drew near to this place, Moffat directed his men to take his waggon to the valley below while he walked towards the house, which was situated on an eminence. As he advanced the farmer came forward slowly to meet him. Stretching forth his hand with the customary salutation, the farmer put his hand behind him, and asked who the stranger was. The stranger replied that he was Moffat.

"Moffat!" exclaimed the sturdy Boer in a faltering voice, "it is your ghost!"

"I am no ghost," said the supposed phantom.

"Don't come near me," said the farmer, "you have been long since murdered by Africaner. Everybody says you were murdered, and a man told me he had seen your bones."

As the farmer feared the presence of the supposed ghost would alarm his wife, both wended their way to the waggon, Africaner being the subject of conversation as they walked along. Moffat declared his opinion that the chief was then a truly good man.

"I can believe almost anything you say," said the Boer, "but that I cannot credit."

Finally he closed the conversation by saying with much earnestness: "Well, if what you assert be true respecting that man, I have only one wish, and that is to see him before I die, and when you return, as sure as the sun is over our heads, I will go with you to see him, though he killed my own uncle."

The farmer was a good man, who had showed Moffat kindness on his way to Namaqualand. Knowing his sincerity and the goodness of his disposition, Moffat turned to the man sitting by the waggon, and addressing the farmer said, "This, then, is Africaner."

With a start, and a look as though the man might have dropped from the clouds, the worthy Boer exclaimed, "Are *you* Africaner?"

Africaner arose, doffed his old hat, and making a polite bow replied, "I am."

The farmer seemed thunderstruck, but on realising the fact, lifted up his eyes and said, "O God, what a miracle of Thy power! what cannot Thy grace accomplish!"

On reaching Cape Town, Robert Moffat waited upon Lord Charles Somerset, the Governor, and informed him that Africaner was in the town. The information was received with some amount of scepticism, but the following day was appointed for an interview with him.

The Governor received the chief with great affability and kindness, and expressed his pleasure at thus seeing before him, one who had formerly been the scourge of the country, and the terror of the border colonists. He was much struck with this palpable result of missionary enterprise, and presented Africaner with an excellent waggon, valued at eighty pounds.

Moffat visited the colony on this occasion with two objects; first, to secure supplies, and secondly, to introduce Africaner to the notice of the Colonial Government. Having accomplished these, he fully intended to return to his flock. Events were, however, ordered otherwise.

While Moffat was in Cape Town, a deputation from the London Missionary Society, consisting of the Rev. J. Campbell, and the Rev. Dr. Philip, was also there. It was the wish of these two gentleman that he should accompany them in their visits to the missionary stations, and eventually be appointed to the Bechwana mission.

The proposition was a startling one, but after careful thought, and with the entire concurrence of Africaner—who hoped to move with his tribe to the neighbourhood of the new mission—Moffat accepted it. Africaner therefore departed alone, generously offering to take in his waggon to Lattakoo, the new station, the missionary's books and a few articles of furniture that he had purchased.

Once more these two brethren in the faith met on this earth, and this was at Lattakoo. The proposed removal of the tribe, however, never took place, Africaner being called up higher before that plan could be carried out.

The closing scene in the life of this remarkable man was depicted by the Rev. J. Archbell, Wesleyan missionary, in a letter to Dr. Philip, dated the 14th of March, 1823:—"When he found his end approaching, he called all the people together, and gave them directions as to their future conduct. 'We are not,' said he, 'what we were,—*savages*, but men professing to be taught according to the Gospel. Let us then do accordingly. Live peaceably with all men, if possible; and if impossible, consult those who are placed over you before you engage in anything. Remain together, as you have done since I knew you. Then, when the Directors think fit to send you a missionary, you may be ready to receive him. Behave to any teacher you may have sent as one sent of God, as I have great hope that God will bless you in this respect when I am gone to heaven. I feel that I love God, and that He has done much for me, of which I am totally unworthy,'

"He also added, 'My former life is stained with blood; but Jesus Christ has pardoned me, and I am going to heaven. Oh! beware of falling into the same evils into which I have led you frequently; but seek God, and He will be found of you to direct you,'"

Shortly after this he died.

CHAPTER IV
MARRIAGE, AND ARRIVAL AT LATTAKOO

Up to this time, Robert Moffat had pursued his course alone. No loving helpmeet had cheered him in his efforts, or with womanly tenderness ministered to his wants. But though far away, he was fondly remembered and earnestly prayed for, especially by one noble Christian lady, over whose fair head scarce twenty-three summers had passed, and whose heart had been torn with the severe struggle, between filial love and regard for her parents on the one hand, and her sense of duty and affection for her missionary friend on the other, which for two and a-half years had been carried on therein.

At last, when hope seemed to have vanished, the parents of Mary Smith, to whom the idea of parting with their only daughter was painful in the extreme, saw so clearly that it was the Lord who was calling their child to the work which He had marked out for her, that they felt they dare not any longer withhold her from it, and therefore calmly resigned their daughter into His hands. Thus it came to pass that,—after a short stay in London, and at Cowes, in the Isle of Wight, at which places she won all hearts by her unfeigned and exalted piety and zeal, and by her modest, affectionate manner,—we find her on board the sailing-ship *British Colony*, on her way to South Africa, in the care of the Rev. R. Beck, a minister of the Dutch Church, and his wife.

As arranged, the deputation, accompanied by Robert Moffat, left Cape Town on their tour of inspection of the stations in the eastern part of the Colony and in Kafirland. This journey necessitated an absence of twelve months, during which time Robert expected his bride to arrive. This was a trial of faith, as it seemed hard that she should be obliged to land in a strange country, and find none of her own to welcome her. But with Moffat even love followed after duty.

It so happened, however, that after visiting the line of stations through the eastern districts as far as Bethelsdorp, the party, at that place, found their progress effectually barred through war with the Kafirs. They were therefore obliged to return to Cape Town, thus giving Moffat the opportunity and great joy of receiving his affianced wife upon her landing from the vessel. She reached Cape Town in safety, and on the 27th of December, 1819, the happy couple were united. They received each other as from the Lord, and for more than fifty years, during cloud and sunshine, their union was a true and blessed one.

Robert Moffat had been appointed to the Bechwana station at Lattakoo, or Kuruman, as it was afterwards called; and for that place the missionary party, which consisted of the Rev. John Campbell and the Moffats, set out early in the year 1820.

A feeble attempt to establish a mission to the Bechwanas had been made, by the Dutch Missionary Society in Cape Town, as early as A.D. 1800, and two missionaries, named Edwards and Kok, had been despatched. They were directed by the chief to settle on the banks of the Kuruman River, at a distance from the natives, and the effort degenerated into a mere trading concern. In 1805, the Bechwanas were visited by the celebrated traveller Dr. Lichtenstein, and, in 1812, by Dr. Burchell, but it was not until the visit of the Rev. J. Campbell, a little later, that any real negotiations were entertained for the settlement of missionaries with this people. The chief, Mothibi, then said to Mr. Campbell, "send missionaries, and I will be a father to them."

In response to this invitation Messrs. Evans and Hamilton left England in 1815, and, full of hope, reached Lattakoo on the 17th of February in the following year. Instead of being received as they anticipated, they were repulsed, and directed to settle at the Kuruman River, thirty miles distant. Disappointed and despondent they returned to Griqua Town. Mr. Evans relinquished the mission, but a further attempt was made afterwards by Messrs. Read and Hamilton, and this time permission was obtained for them to dwell with the chief and his people. Thus the Bechwana Mission obtained its first real footing.

In June, 1817, the tribe, under Mothibi, removed from the position where the missionaries first found it, and settled by the Kuruman River. When the Rev. J. Campbell returned, to the Colony, Mr. Read accompanied him; thus, pending the arrival of Robert Moffat, Mr. Hamilton was left alone in charge of the mission.

The journey as far as Griqua Town was accomplished without any special incident. At first the route lay through fertile valleys and lovely mountain scenery, but soon this changed, and for hundreds of miles the travellers had to pass through the desolate region of the Karroo desert. When about half-way through this sterile district, they came to the site upon which was to be built the village of Beaufort West, where they were most kindly entertained by a Scotchman named Mr. Baird, the newly appointed magistrate.

The Orange River, so frequently an insurmountable obstacle to progress, was passed in safety, the water being very low, and two or three days later Griqua Town was reached. Here a halt was made. Lattakoo lay one hundred miles beyond.

At this time some uncertainty existed as to whether the Moffats would be allowed by the Colonial Government to settle at Lattakoo; thus far consent had been withheld. They had advanced trusting that the way would be opened, and after a short rest at Griqua Town, the party continued their journey, and reached Lattakoo five days after leaving the Griqua station. It was intended that Robert Moffat should take the place of Mr. Read, as an associate with Mr. Hamilton in the work of the mission.

The new arrivals were introduced to Mothibi, and were soon visited by a retinue of chiefs. The manner, appearance, and dress of these natives much interested Mary Moffat. The whole missionary party stayed together for three weeks, settling the affairs of the mission; then the Rev. J. Campbell and Mr. Read started on a journey to visit the Bahurutsi, a tribe who dwelt nearly two hundred miles to the northeast of Lattakoo. Moffat and his wife remained with Mr. Hamilton, so that the new missionary might win the affections of the Bechwana chief and his people.

Upon the return of the Rev. J. Campbell and Mr. Read, after an absence of two months, and a short rest at Lattakoo, all the missionaries, excepting Mr. Hamilton, set off westward along the bed of the Kuruman River to visit several of the Bechwana tribes which were scattered about that region. The natives of these parts, never having seen white people before evinced much curiosity concerning their visitors; especially about Mrs. Moffat and her dress. To see the missionaries sitting at table dining and using knives and forks, plates, and different dishes, was wonderful to them, and for hours they would sit and gaze upon such scenes.

The Word of Life was preached to these natives by either Mr. Campbell or Robert Moffat as the party journeyed along.

Their absence from Lattakoo extended to a little over a fortnight, and on their return, finding, by intelligence received from Dr. Philip, that permission had not as yet been obtained from the Governor for the Moffats to settle at that place, Robert and his partner had to return, much cast down, to Griqua Town, there to commit the matter into the hand of God, and patiently await the time when He should open the way for them to commence the work they had so much at heart. Mr. Hamilton was therefore again left alone with simply a Griqua assistant and a few Hottentots.

Just before leaving Lattakoo, Robert Moffat met Africaner, who had safely brought from Vreede Berg the cattle and property belonging to the missionary, and also the books and articles of furniture which had been intrusted to his care when leaving Cape Town. All were in good order, particular attention having been paid to the missionary's cattle and sheep during his long absence. This was the last meeting between Moffat and Africaner.

While on their journey, and when near Griqua Town, information reached the missionary party that permission had been granted for the Moffats to settle at Lattakoo. As, however, the affairs at Griqua Town at this time were altogether disorganised, it was arranged that they should stay there for a few months to set the affairs of that place in order.

During their stay at that station Mrs. Moffat had a severe illness, and her life was despaired of, but this precious life was preserved, and not only was his dear one restored, but a bonny wee lassie was given to them both, who was named Mary, and who, in after years, became the wife of Dr. Livingstone.

At Griqua Town they bade farewell to the Rev. J. Campbell. To them he had become much endeared, as they had been in his company as fellow-travellers for many months. He and Mr. Read returned to the Colony; twenty years later, however, the two friends met again, but that was upon the Moffats' return to their native land.

In May, 1821, Mr. and Mrs. Moffat again arrived at Lattakoo, and then commenced a continuation of missionary conflicts during which their faith was severely tried, but which ended, after many years, in triumphant rejoicing as they saw the people brought to Christ, and beheld the once ignorant and degraded heathen becoming humble servants of the Lord, reading His Word and obeying His precepts.

In looking at the Bechwanas as they were when the Moffats first settled among them, for up to that time the efforts of the missionaries had been unattended with success, we find a people who had neither an idea of a God, nor who performed any idolatrous rites; who failed to see that there was anything more agreeable to flesh and blood in our customs than in their own; but who allowed that the missionaries were a wiser and superior race of beings to themselves; who practised polygamy, and looked with a very jealous eye on any innovation that was likely to deprive them of the services of their wives, who built their houses, gathered firewood for their fires, tilled their fields, and reared their families; who were suspicious, and keenly scrutinised the actions of the missionaries; in fact, a people who were thoroughly

OLD MISSION HOUSE AT GRIQUA TOWN.

sensual, and who could rob, lie, and murder without any compunctions of conscience, as long as success attended their efforts.

Among such a people did these servants of God labour for years without any
sign of fruit, but with steadfast faith and persevering prayer, until at last the work
of the Holy Spirit was seen, and the strong arm of the Lord, gathering many into
His fold, became apparent.

The Bechwana tribe with whom Robert Moffat was located was called the
Batlaping, or Batlapis.

The patience of the missionaries in these early days was sorely tried, and the
petty annoyances, so irritating to many of us, were neither few nor infrequent. By

dint of immense labour, leading the water to it, the ground which the chief had given the missionaries for a garden was made available; then the women, headed by the chief's wife, encroached upon it, and to save contention the point was conceded. The corn when it ripened was stolen, and the sheep either taken out of the fold at night or driven off when grazing in the day time. No tool or household utensil could be left about for a moment or it would disappear.

One day Mr. Hamilton, who at that time had no mill to grind corn, sat down and with much labour and perspiration, by means of two stones, ground sufficient meal in half-a-day to make a loaf that should serve him, being then alone, for about eight days. He kneaded and baked his gigantic loaf, put it on his shelf, and went to the chapel. He returned in the evening with a keen appetite and a pleasant anticipation of enjoying his coarse home-made bread, but on opening the door of his hut and casting his eye to the shelf he saw that the loaf had gone. Someone had forced open the little window of the hut, got in, and stolen the bread.

On another occasion Mrs. Moffat, with a babe in her arms, begged very humbly of a woman, just to be kind enough to move out of a temporary kitchen, that she might shut it as usual before going into the place of worship. The woman seized a piece of wood to hurl at Mrs. Moffat's head, who, therefore, escaped to the house of God, leaving the intruder in undisturbed possession of the kitchen, any of the contents of which she would not hesitate to appropriate to her own use.

A severe drought also set in, and a rain-maker, finding all his arts to bring rain useless, laid the blame upon the white strangers, who for a time were in expectation of being driven away. Probably, however, the greatest trial at this time was caused by the conduct of some of the Hottentots who had accompanied them from the Cape, and who being but new converts were weak to withstand the demands made upon them, and brought shame upon their leaders. Shortly after his arrival Moffat thoroughly purged his little community. The numbers that gathered round the Lord's table were much reduced, but the lesson was a salutary one and did good to the heathen around.

A callous indifference to the instruction of the missionaries, except it was followed by some temporal benefit, prevailed. In August, 1822, Mary Moffat wrote, "We have no prosperity in the work, not the least sign of good being done. The Bechwanas seem more careless than ever, and seldom enter the church." A little later Moffat himself stated in one of his letters, "They turn a deaf ear to the voice of love, and treat with scorn the glorious doctrines of salvation. It is, however, pleasing to reflect that affairs in general wear a more hopeful aspect than when we came here. Several instances have proved the people are determined to relinquish the barbarous system of commandoes for stealing cattle. They have also dispensed with a rain-maker this season."

The Bushmen had a most inhuman custom of abandoning the aged and helpless, leaving them to starve or be devoured by wild beasts; also if a mother died it was their practice to bury the infant or infants of that mother with her.

During one of his journeys, a few months prior to the date last mentioned, Moffat came upon a party of Bushmen digging a grave for the body of a woman who had left two children. Finding that they were about to bury the children with the corpse he begged for them. They were given him and for some years formed a part of his household. They were named Ann and Dicky.

The importance of acquiring the language of the Bechwanas soon became apparent to the earnest-hearted missionary. One day he was much cast down and said to his wife, "Mary, this is hard work." "It is hard work, my love," she replied, "but take courage, our lives shall be given us for a prey." "But think, my dear," he said, "how long we have been preaching to this people, and no fruit yet appears." The wise woman made answer, "The Gospel has not yet been preached to them *in their own tongue in which they were born*. They have heard it only through interpreters, and interpreters who have themselves no just understanding, no real love of the truth. We must not expect the blessing till you are able, from your own lips and in their language, to bring it through their ears into their hearts."

"From that hour," said Moffat, in relating the conversation, "I gave myself with untiring diligence to the acquisition of the language."

As an instance of the drawback of preaching by means of an interpreter, the sentence, "The salvation of the soul is a very important subject," was rendered by one of those individuals as follows: "The salvation of the soul is a very great sack." A rendering altogether unintelligible.

For the purpose of studying the language Moffat made journeys among the tribes, so that he might for a time be freed from speaking Dutch, the language spoken with his own people at Lattakoo. Itinerating visits were also made in turn every

Sabbath to the surrounding villages, and occasionally further afield, but sometimes, after walking perhaps four to five miles to reach a village, not a single individual could be found to listen to the Gospel message.

The only service in which the missionaries took any real delight at this time, was the Sabbath evening service held in Dutch for the edification of themselves and the two or three Hottentots, with their families, who belonged to the mission.

In addition to sore privations, discouragements, false accusations, and the loss of their property, the missionaries found even their lives at times imperilled. The natives and all on the station were suffering greatly from a long continued drought. All the efforts of the professional rain-maker had been in vain, no cloud appeared in the sky, no rain fell to water the parched land. The doings of the missionaries were looked upon as being the cause of this misfortune. At one time it was a bag of salt, which Moffat had brought in his waggon, that frightened the rain away; at another the sound of the chapel bell. Their prospects became darker than ever. At last it appeared that the natives had fully decided to expel them from their midst. A chief man, and about a dozen of his attendants, came and seated themselves under the shadow of a large tree near to Moffat's house. He at that moment was engaged in repairing a waggon near at hand. The scene which ensued and its result we give in his own words:—

"Being informed that something of importance was to be communicated, Mr. Hamilton was called. We stood patiently to hear the message, always ready to face the worst. The principal speaker informed us, that it was the determination of the chiefs of the people that we should leave the country; and referring to our disregard of threatenings, added what was tantamount to the assurance that measures of a violent character would be resorted to, to carry their resolutions into effect, in case of our disobeying the order.

"While the chief was speaking, he stood quivering his spear in his right hand. Mrs. Moffat was at the door of our cottage, with the babe in her arms, watching the crisis, for such it was. We replied:—

"'We have indeed felt most reluctant to leave, and are now more than ever resolved to abide by our post. We pity you, for you know not what you do; we have suffered, it is true; and He whose servants we are has directed us in His Word,

"NOW THEN, IF YOU WILL DRIVE YOUR SPEARS TO MY HEART."

"When they persecute you in one city, flee ye to another," but although we have suffered, we do not consider all that has been done to us by the people amounts to persecution; we are prepared to expect it from such as know no better. If you are resolved to rid yourselves of us, you must resort to stronger measures, for our hearts are with you. You may shed blood or burn us out. We know you will not touch our wives and children."'

Then throwing open his waistcoat Moffat stood erect and fearless. "Now then," said he, "if you will, drive your spears to my heart; and when you have slain me, my companions will know that the hour has come for them to depart."

At these words the chief man looked at his companions, remarking, with a significant shake of the head, "These men must have ten lives, when they are so fearless of death; there must be something in immortality."

Moffat pithily observes, "The meeting broke up, and they left us, no doubt fully impressed with the idea that we were impracticable men."

CHAPTER V
THE MANTATEE INVASION

In March, 1823, a second daughter was born to the Moffats, who was named Ann. At that time the Batlaping were thoroughly indifferent to the Gospel, but their hostile spirit to the missionaries had passed away.

Robert Moffat had heard of a powerful Bechwana tribe, named the Bangwaketsi, whose chief was Makaba, dwelling about two hundred miles to the north-east. To this chief and people he now contemplated paying a visit.

Rumours had also been current at intervals, for more than a year past, of strange and terrible doings by a fierce and numerous people, called the Mantatees, who were advancing from the eastward. To gain definite intelligence concerning this people, and also with the view of paying his contemplated visit to Makaba, Moffat resolved upon undertaking a journey to that chief. He was also influenced by the desire to open up a friendly intercourse with so powerful, and it might be dangerous, a potentate as Makaba; and likewise by the wish of gaining opportunities of more fully studying the language and becoming acquainted with the localities of the tribes; the ultimate design of all being the introduction of the Gospel among them.

An invitation arrived from Makaba, and the way seemed open. Mothibi, however, the Bechwana chief, was greatly averse to the undertaking, and threw all possible obstacles in its path, short of actual armed resistance. His people were forbidden to accompany the missionary, who was obliged therefore to start with only the few men he had.

As he journeyed forward the reports concerning the Mantatees were again heard, and on reaching Nokaneng, about twenty miles distant from Lattakoo, he learned that the invaders had attacked a Bechwana tribe, the Barolongs, at Kunuana, about one hundred miles off. Spies were sent out but returned without any definite tidings, and the journey was resumed.

For four days the party travelled across a dry and trackless country, when they came to a fine valley, in which were some pools and plenty of game. Here they remained two days, and then prepared to continue their journey to the Bangwaketsi. Just as they were about to start, however, they ascertained from two natives that the Mantatees had attacked the Barolongs, and were in possession of a village somewhat in the rear of the missionary's party.

No time was to be lost. The distance was retraced with all speed, and the alarming news told at Lattakoo. A public meeting was convened, and Moffat gave a circumstantial account of the information he had gathered. The enemy were a numerous and powerful body, they had destroyed many towns of the Bakone tribes, slaughtered immense numbers of people, laid Kurrechane in ruins, scattered the Barolongs, and, in addition, were said to be cannibals.

The alarming tidings produced at first, a gloom on every countenance, and silence reigned for a few minutes. Then Mothibi, in the name of the assembly, said he was exceedingly thankful that their missionary had been "hard-headed" and pursued his journey, thus discovering to them their danger.

Moffat counselled that as the Bechwanas were quite unable to resist so savage a force as the Mantatees, they had better either flee to the Colony or call in the aid of the Griquas, volunteering to proceed to Griqua Town to give information and procure assistance. The chief at that place was one Andries Waterboer, who had been educated by the missionaries, and who, before his election as chief, had been set apart for a native teacher. Mr. Melville, the Government agent, also resided in the town.

Moffat reached Griqua Town safely, and Waterboer promised to come to the assistance of the Bechwanas as soon as he could muster his forces. Moffat then returned to his station.

Eleven anxious days were passed at Lattakoo, waiting the arrival of the Griquas. By the time they arrived, the enemy had reached Letakong, only thirty-six miles away. The Griqua force consisted of about one hundred horsemen, armed with guns, and it being reported that there were white men among the invaders, Moffat was asked to accompany the force, as, having some knowledge of the language, he might be able to bring about a treaty with them. He agreed to go, and Mr. Melville started with him.

Before leaving, all met to pray for Divine counsel and help. A blessing on the means of preventing a further effusion of blood was asked, and if recourse to violent measures became necessary, it was prayed that the heads of those engaged might be shielded in the day of battle.

The small force pressed forward as far as the Matlaurin River, about half way, where all bivouacked. Leaving the main body, Waterboer, Moffat, and a few others, rode onward for about four hours, and then halted for the night among some trees. At day-light they proceeded until they came in sight of the enemy. These were divided into two parties, one holding a town, out of which they had driven the inhabitants, and the other lying on the hills to the left of the town. As the horsemen drew near, they could perceive that they were discovered, and among the masses of the invaders could be seen the war-axes and brass ornaments as they glittered in the sun.

Riding forward, Moffat and Waterboer found a young woman belonging to the Mantatees, whose whole appearance denoted direful want. Food was given her, and some tobacco, and she was sent with a message to her people that the strangers wanted to speak with them and not to fight. An old man and a lad were also found dying of starvation, these were helped and talked to in full sight of the enemy. All possible means were tried to bring them to a parley, but in vain, they only responded by making furious rushes, showing their intention to attack.

The whole day was spent in this manner, and at evening Moffat left Waterboer and the scouts, and rode back to confer with Mr. Melville and the other Griqua chiefs, to see if some means could be devised of preventing the dreadful consequences of battle. One of the Griqua chiefs, named Cornelius Kok, nobly insisted on Moffat taking his best horse, one of the strongest present. To this generous act the missionary afterwards owed his life.

All the party were in motion the next morning before day-light. The whole of the horsemen advanced to within about one hundred and fifty yards of the enemy, thinking to intimidate them and bring them to a conference. The Mantatees rushed forward with a terrible howl, throwing their war clubs and javelins. The rushes becoming dangerous, Waterboer and his party commenced firing, and the battle became general. The Mantatees obstinately held their ground, seeming determined rather to perish than flee, which they might easily have done.

After the combat had lasted two hours and a-half, the Griquas, finding their ammunition rapidly diminishing, advanced to take the enemy's position. The latter gave way and fled, at first westward, but being intercepted, they turned towards the town. Here a desperate struggle took place. At last, seized with despair, the enemy fled precipitately, and were pursued by the Griquas for about eight miles.

Soon after the battle commenced, the Bechwanas who accompanied the Griqua force came up, and began discharging their poisoned arrows into the midst of the Mantatees. Half-a-dozen of these fierce warriors, however, turned upon them, and the whole body scampered off in wild disorder. But as soon as these cowards saw that the Mantatees had retired, they rushed like hungry wolves to the spot where they had been encamped, and began to plunder and kill the wounded, also murdering the women and children with their spears and battle-axes.

Fighting not being within the missionary's province, he refrained from firing a shot, though for safety he kept with the Griqua force. Seeing now the savage ferocity of the Bechwanas in killing the inoffensive women and children, he turned his attention to these objects of pity, who were fleeing in all directions. Galloping in among them, many of the Bechwanas were deterred from their barbarous purpose, and the women, seeing that mercy was shown them, sat down, and baring their breasts, exclaimed, "I am a woman; I am a woman." The men seemed as though it was impossible to yield, and although often sorely wounded, they continued to throw their spears and war-axes at any one who approached.

It was while carrying on his work of mercy among the wounded that Moffat nearly lost his life. He had got hemmed in between a rocky height and a body of the enemy. A narrow passage remained, through which he could escape at full gallop. Right in the middle of this passage there rose up before him a man who had been shot, but who had collected his strength, and, weapon in hand, was awaiting him. Just at that moment one of the Griquas, seeing the situation, fired. The ball whizzed past, close to Moffat. The aim had been a true one, and the way of escape was clear.

This battle saved the mission. It did more than that—it saved the Mantatees themselves from terrible destruction. As a devastating host they would in all probability have advanced to the borders of the Colony, and being driven back, would

have perished miserably, men, women, and children, either of starvation, or at
the hands of those tribes whom they would have overcome in their advance, and
through whose territories they must have passed in their retreat.

After the battle was over, Mr. Melville and Robert Moffat collected many
of the Mantatee women and children, who were taken to the missionary station.
Alarm prevailed there for some days, it being feared that the Mantatees might make
a descent upon the place after the Griquas had left. At one time the prospect was
so ominous that the missionary band, with their wives and children, after burying
their property, left Lattakoo for a short time, and sought shelter at Griqua Town.
The threatened attack not being made, and as it was found that the Mantatees had
left the neighbourhood, the station was again occupied.

The Bechwanas were deeply sensible of the interest the missionaries had shown
in their welfare, at a time when they might with ease and little loss of property
have retired in safety to the Colony, leaving them to be destroyed by the fierce
invaders.

For a long time past, it had been evident to Moffat that the site upon which
they dwelt at Lattakoo was altogether unsuitable for missionary purposes. The great
scarcity of water, especially in dry seasons, rendered any attempt at raising crops
most difficult, and even water for drinking purposes could only be obtained in small
quantity. Advantage was therefore taken of the present favourable impression, made
upon the minds of Mothibi and his people, to obtain a site for a new station. A place
eight miles distant, about three miles below the Kuruman fountain, where the river
of that name had its source, was examined and found to offer better advantages for
a missionary station than any other for hundreds of miles round. Arrangements
were made with the Bechwana chiefs so that about two miles of the Kuruman valley should henceforth be the property of the London Missionary Society, proper
remuneration being given as soon as Moffat returned from Cape Town, to which
place he contemplated paying a visit shortly.

This new station will be known in the further chronicle of events, by the name
of Kuruman.

At the beginning of 1824, the Moffats were in Cape Town. They had gone there
to obtain supplies, to seek medical aid for Mrs. Moffat, who had suffered in health
considerably, and to confer personally with Dr. Philip about the removal of the

station. Mothibi having been anxious that his son, Peclu, should see the country of the white people, had sent him, accompanied by Taisho, one of the principal chiefs, to Cape Town with the missionaries.

The young prince and his companion were astonished at what they saw. With difficulty they were persuaded to go along with Robert Moffat on board one of the ships in the bay. The enormous size of the hull, the height of the masts, the splendid cabin and the deep hold, were each and all objects of wonder; and when they saw a boy mount the rigging and ascend to the masthead, their astonishment was complete. Turning to the young prince, Taisho whispered, "Ah ga si khatla?" (Is it not an ape?) "Do these water-houses (ships) unyoke like waggon-oxen every night?" they inquired; and also; "Do they graze in the sea to keep them alive?" Being asked what they thought of a ship in full sail, which was then entering the harbour, they replied, "We have no thoughts here, we hope to think again when we get on shore."

Upon the same day that the Moffats reached Cape Town, a ship arrived from England, bringing three new missionaries intended for the Bechwana station. Of these, however, one only and his wife, Mr. and Mrs. Hughes, were able to accompany the older missionary upon his return to his post.

Mrs. Moffat's health being somewhat improved, the party left Cape Town, and after a tedious and monotonous journey of two months, Robert and Mary Moffat reached Lattakoo in safety. They had left Mr. and Mrs. Hughes at Griqua Town, where they were to remain for a season. Upon reaching home Mr. Hamilton was found pursuing his lonely labours with that quiet patience so characteristic of him.

CHAPTER VI
VISIT TO MAKABA

Shortly after his return, and pending the final arrangements for the removal of the missionary station, it was considered advisable that Robert Moffat should pay his long promised visit to Makaba, the chief of the Bangwaketsi. He left on the 1st of July, 1824, and was accompanied by a large party of Griquas, who were going into that region to hunt elephants.

Skirting the edge of the Kalahari desert for some time they afterwards deviated from their course through want of water, and visited Pitsana, where a great concourse of natives had gathered, consisting of the different sections of the Barolong tribe, who had been driven from their country the previous year during the invasion of the Mantatees. Thence they proceeded onward till they reached Kwakwe, the residence of Makaba and his people, and the metropolis of the Bangwaketsi. Here the missionary was most favourably received by the king, who remarked, with a laugh, "That he wondered they should trust themselves, unarmed, in the town of such a *villain* as he was reported to be."

He entertained Moffat and his party royally, declaring, "My friends, I am perfectly happy; my heart is whiter than milk, because you have visited me. To-day I am a great man. You are wise and bold to come and see with your own eyes, and laugh at the testimony of my enemies."

Moffat tried on several occasions to converse with the chief and his people on Divine things, but apparently with little success. At length on the Sabbath he resolved to pay Makaba a formal visit, so as to obtain a hearing for the subject. He found the monarch seated among a large number of his principal men, all engaged either preparing skins, cutting them, sewing mantles, or telling news.

NATIVES SEWING.

Sitting down beside him, and amidst his nobles and counsellors, Moffat stated that his object was to tell him news. The missionary spoke of God, of the Saviour, but his words fell upon deaf ears. One of the men sitting near, however, seemed struck with the character of the Redeemer, and especially with His miracles. On hearing that He had raised the dead, the man said, "What an excellent doctor He must have been to raise the dead." This led to a description of His power, and how that power would be exercised at the last day in the Resurrection. The ear of the monarch caught the sound of a resurrection from the dead, "What," he exclaimed in astonishment, "What are these words about? the dead, the dead arise!"

"Yes, all the dead shall arise."

"Will my father arise?"

"Yes, your father will arise."

"Will all the slain in battle arise?"

"Yes."

"And will all that have been killed and devoured by lions, tigers, hyenas, and crocodiles again revive?"

"Yes; and come to judgment."

"And will those whose bodies have been left to waste and to wither on the desert plains and scattered to the winds again arise?" asked the king, with a kind of triumph, as though this time he had fixed the missionary.

"Yes!" answered he, with emphasis; "not one will be left behind."

After looking at his visitor for a few moments, Makaba turned to his people, saying in a stentorian voice: "Hark, ye wise men, whoever is among you, the wisest of past generations, did ever your ears hear such strange and unheard-of news?"

Receiving an answer in the negative, he laid his hand upon Moffat's breast and said, "Father, I love you much. Your visit and your presence have made my heart as white as milk. The words of your mouth are sweet as honey, but the words of a resurrection are too great to be heard. I do not wish to hear again about the dead rising! The dead cannot arise! The dead must not arise!"

"Why," inquired the missionary, "can so great a man refuse knowledge and turn away from wisdom? Tell me, my friend, why I must not add to words and speak of a resurrection?"

Raising and uncovering his arm which had been strong in battle, and shaking his hand as if quivering a spear, he replied, "I have slain my thousands, and shall they arise!"

"Never before," adds Mr. Moffat in his ***Missionary Labours***, "had the light of Divine revelation dawned upon his savage mind, and of course his conscience had never accused him, no, not for one of the thousands of deeds of rapine and murder which had marked his course through a long career."

Starting homewards, the Griqua hunting party, for some altogether unexplained reason, announced their intention of returning with the missionary instead of remaining behind to hunt; a most providential circumstance, which in all probability saved the lives of Moffat and his followers and many more besides.

A few hours after leaving Makaba, messengers met the returning company from Tauane, the chief of the Barolongs, asking the help of the missionary party as he was about to be attacked by the Mantatees. On reaching Pitsana they found that such was the case. The attack was made and repelled by the Griquas, about twenty in number, mounted and armed with guns; and thus the town was saved, the flight of its inhabitants into the Kalahari desert, there to perish of hunger and thirst, prevented, and the safety of Robert Moffat and his companions secured.

The time during which Moffat had been absent from Lattakoo, had been a most anxious one for his wife and those who remained at the station. A band of marauders had gathered in the Long Mountains, about forty miles to the westward, and after attacking some villages on the Kuruman, had threatened an attack on the Batlaping and the mission premises. The dreaded Mantatees were also reported to be in the neighbourhood. One night when Mary Moffat was alone with her little ones and the two Bushmen children, Mr. Hamilton and the assistants being away at the new station, a loud rap came at the door, and inquiring who was there, Mothibi himself replied. He brought word that the Mantatees were approaching.

A hasty message was sent to Mr. Hamilton, who arrived about eight o'clock in the morning when preparations were made for flight. Messengers continued to arrive, each bringing tidings that caused fresh alarm, until about noon, when it was ascertained that the fierce and savage enemy had turned aside and directed their course to the Barolongs.

The station was safe, but the loving heart of the missionary's wife was torn with anguish, as she foresaw that the dreaded Mantatees would be crossing her husband's path just at the time when he, almost alone, was returning on his homeward way.

Prayer was the support of Mary Moffat under this terrible ordeal, and the way prayer was answered has been seen, in the unaccountable manner in which Berend Berend and his party of Griquas changed their minds and resolved upon returning with Robert Moffat, instead of remaining to hunt elephants in the country of the Bangwaketsi.

The remainder of the year 1824 witnessed bloodshed and strife all around. War among the Bechwanas, attacks by the marauders of the Long Mountains, commotions among the interior tribes: the land was deluged with blood; even the warlike Bangwaketsi were dispersed, and Makaba was killed. Once again the missionaries had to flee with their families to Griqua Town, leaving Mr. Hamilton, as he was without family in charge of the new station, with two horses ready for flight in case of danger.

The end of the year found the Kuruman missionaries,—who now consisted of Robert and Mary Moffat, Mr. and Mrs. Hughes, and Mr. Hamilton,—with the exception of the last named, at Griqua Town.

The new station at the Kuruman had been occupied shortly before the departure of the fugitives; and early in 1825, finding that the immediate danger had passed, the Moffats, accompanied by Mr. and Mrs. Hughes, rejoined Mr. Hamilton. Two events of a distressing character to the Batlaping and their missionaries occurred about this time. The first was the passage of two terrible hail-storms over a portion of the country, destroying the crops, killing lambs, and stripping the bark from trees. The second was the death of the young prince, Peclu, who had an excellent disposition, was comparatively enlightened, and whose influence the missionaries expected would have been most salutary among his countrymen.

This sorrowful event, combined with a further attack upon the Batlaping by the marauders, determined Mothibi and his people to leave their present place of settlement and remove to the eastward. For a considerable time, however, they remained in an unsettled state, suffering from attacks, and leading a vagrant life.

The work of laying out the new station was proceeded with. Three temporary dwellings had already been erected, consisting of a wooden framework, filled up with reeds, and plastered within and without; the foundations of more permanent dwellings had also been laid. Mr. Hughes, who had been to Cape Town for supplies, returned, accompanied by a mason named Millen and a few Hottentot assistants from Bethelsdorp. The company at the station was a large one, and to provide them with food was a work of difficulty.

The Kuruman fountain, the source of the Kuruman river, issues from caverns in a little hill. It was the purpose of the missionaries to lead the water from the river to irrigate their gardens. For this purpose a trench was cut two miles in length. This was a work of great labour and was attended by considerable danger. It was found necessary that the men when working should have their guns with them, in case of being surprised by the robbers who roved about. Moffat says, "it was dug in troublous times."

Sickness and death entered the missionary dwellings. An infant son was born to the Moffats, and five days after called away. Mr. Hughes was laid low through a severe cold, and brought to the gates of death. When all hope seemed to have vanished he began to amend, though his health was not restored until he and Mrs. Hughes made a journey to the Cape. In 1827 he left Kuruman and removed to the Griqua Mission. The mother of Mary Moffat died in October, 1825, but the news did not reach her daughter in Africa until April, 1826.

Referring to this time Robert Moffat says: "Our situation during the infancy of the new station, I shall not attempt to describe. Some of our newly arrived assistants, finding themselves in a country where the restraints of law were unknown, and not being under the influence of religion, would not submit to the privations which we patiently endured, but murmured exceedingly. Armed robbers were continually making inroads, threatening death and extirpation. We were compelled to work daily at every species of labour, most of which was very heavy, under a burning sun, and in a dry climate, where only one shower had fallen during the preceding twelve months. These are only imperfect samples of our engagements for several years at the new station, while at the same time, the language, which was entirely oral, had to be acquired."

Notwithstanding all the impediments to such an enterprise, Robert Moffat had made some progress towards establishing a literature in the native, or Sechwana tongue. A spelling-book, catechism, and some small portions of Scripture had been prepared, and sent to the Cape to be printed, in 1825. Through a mistake, these were unfortunately sent on to England, causing much disappointment and delay.

Things settled down somewhat in 1826. The discontented Hottentots returned to the Colony, leaving the missionaries and Mr. Millen to carry on the work of laying out the station, erecting the buildings, and the other manual labour connected with the undertaking, assisted only by such poor help as they could get from the Bechwanas.

The native population at the station had been much reduced. Such of the Batlaping as had not moved away, had settled down about the Kuruman valley. They did not oppose the Gospel, but they appeared quite indifferent to it.

For several years the country had been parched through drought, but early in 1826 rain fell plentifully. The earth was soon covered with verdure, but the bright prospects of abundance were quickly cut off. Swarms of locusts infested the land, and vegetation was entirely destroyed. This led to great scarcity, and although the natives caught and ate the locusts, hunger and suffering prevailed. The missionaries' cattle could not be let out of sight, or they were instantly stolen. One day two noted fellows from the mountains pounced down upon a man who had charge of some oxen. They murdered the man and made off with an ox.

To become proficient in the Sechwana language was the earnest purpose of Robert Moffat. At the end of the year 1826, having moved into his new dwelling, built of stone, and the state of the country being somewhat more tranquil, he left his home and family, to sojourn for a time among the Barolongs, so that he might live exclusively with the natives and attend to their speech.

He made the journey by ox-waggon, and was accompanied by the waggon-driver, a boy, and two Barolongs who were journeying to the same place as himself. The dangers attending these journeyings from tribe to tribe were by no means imaginary, the following, related in Moffat's own words, serving as an illustration of some of the perils often encountered:

"The two Barolongs had brought a young cow with them, and though I recommended their making her fast as well as the oxen, they humorously replied that she was too wise to leave the waggon, even though a lion should be scented. We took a little supper, which was followed by our evening hymn and prayer. I had retired only a few minutes to my waggon to prepare for the night, when the whole of the oxen started to their feet. A lion had seized the cow only a few steps from their tails, and dragged it to the distance of thirty or forty yards, where we distinctly heard it tearing the animal and breaking its bones, while its bellowings were most pitiful. When these were over, I seized my gun, but as it was too dark to see half the distance, I aimed at the spot where the devouring jaws of the lion were heard. I fired again and again, to which he replied with tremendous roars, at the same time making a rush towards the waggon so as exceedingly to terrify the oxen. The two Barolongs engaged to take firebrands and throw them at him so as to afford me a degree of light that I might take aim. They had scarcely discharged them from their hands when the flames went out, and the enraged animal rushed towards them with such swiftness, that I had barely time to turn the gun and fire between the men and the lion. The men darted through some thorn bushes with countenances indicative of the utmost terror. It was now the opinion of all that we had better let him alone if he did not molest us.

"Having but a scanty supply of wood to keep up a fire, one man crept among the bushes on one side of the pool, while I proceeded for the same purpose on the other side. I had not gone far, when looking upward to the edge of the small basin, I discerned between me and the sky four animals, whose attention appeared to be directed to me by the noise I made in breaking a dry stick. On closer inspection I found that the large round, hairy-headed visitors were lions, and retreated on my hands and feet towards the other side of the pool, when coming to my waggon-driver, I found him looking with no little alarm in an opposite direction, and with good reason, as no fewer than two lions with a cub were eyeing us both, apparently as uncertain about us as we were distrustful of them. We thankfully decamped to the waggon and sat down to keep alive our scanty fire, while we listened to the lion tearing and devouring his prey. When any of the other hungry lions dared to approach he would pursue them for some paces with a horrible howl, which made our poor oxen tremble, and produced anything but agreeable sensations to ourselves. We had reason for alarm, lest any of the six lions we saw, fearless of our small fire, might rush in among us."

BAROLONG WOMEN.

From these dangers Moffat was mercifully preserved and after journeying for six days he reached the village of a young chief named Bogachu. At this place, and at one about twenty miles distant, he lived a semi-savage life for ten weeks. To use a common expression he "made himself at home" among them. They were kind and appeared delighted with his company, especially as when food run scarce, he could take his gun and shoot a rhinoceros or some other animal, when a night of feasting and talking would follow.

Every opportunity was embraced by the missionary of imparting Christian instruction to these people; their supreme idea of happiness, however, seemed able to rise no higher than having plenty of meat. Asking a man, who seemed more grave than the rest, what was the finest sight he could desire, he replied, "A great fire covered with pots full of meat," adding, "How ugly the fire looks without a pot"

The object of the journey was fully gained; henceforth Robert Moffat needed no interpreter; he could now speak and preach to the people in their own tongue. He found all well on reaching home and prepared to settle down with a feeling of ability to the work of translation.

The prospects of the mission at this time began to brighten. Several thousands of the natives had gathered on the opposite side of the valley, near the mission station. They were becoming more settled in their minds, and would collect in the different divisions of the town when the missionaries visited them; the public attendance at the regular religious services daily increased, and the school was better attended. No visible signs of an inward change in the natives could yet be seen, but Moffat and his fellow-workers felt certain that this was not far off.

War again intervened and darkened the brightening prospects. Once more the missionaries, after prayerful consideration, felt it necessary to flee to Griqua Town, suffering much loss of time and of property. Happily the storm passed over, and, on returning to the Kuruman, they found their houses, and such property as they had left behind, in good order, a proof of the influence they were gaining over the once thievish Bechwanas. Half the oxen and nearly all the cows belonging to the missionaries were, however, dead, no milk could be obtained, and, worse than these evils, the people had fled, leaving their native houses but heaps of ashes.

Sorrowfully these servants of God resolved once more to resume their labours. A few poor natives had remained at the station, whose numbers were being increased by others who arrived from day to day.

At this trying time the hearts of Robert Moffat and his companions were cheered by the arrival of the Rev. Robert Miles, the Society's superintendent, who, having made himself conversant with the affairs of the station, suggested the great importance of preparing something like hymns in the native language. By the continued singing of these, he stated the great truths of salvation would become imperceptibly written on the minds of the people.

The suggestion so kindly made was acted upon, and Moffat prepared the first hymn in the language. The spelling-books also arrived, which enabled the missionaries to open a school in the Sechwana tongue. Mr. Miles returned, and the stated labours of the mission were carried forward. With few interruptions they had been continued for ten years without fruit. But the dawn of a new era seemed now ready to rise above the horizon.

Yet again, however, was their faith to be sorely tried by the terrible scourge— war. The desperadoes consisted this time of a party advancing from the Orange River, among whom were some Griquas. The suspense and anxiety were great, but recourse was had to prayer. On this occasion the missionaries determined to remain at their post. A first attack was repulsed through the intrepidity of an escaped slave named Aaron Josephs, and a peaceful interval intervened of about two months, when a second attack on the mission premises was threatened. By Moffat's directions, the heights at the back of the station were crowded with men, to give the appearance of a large defending force, though probably not a dozen guns could have been mustered among them. The assailants seeing the preparations for defence, drew up at some distance, and, after a short delay, sent forward two messengers with a flag of truce. Moffat went out to meet them, and learned that a renegade Christian Griqua named Jantye Goeman wished to see him at their camp.

A meeting was arranged half way between the station and the camp, and Jantye, who was ashamed to let the missionary see his face, as he had known him at Griqua Town, tried to lay all the blame upon another renegade, a Coranna chief named Paul, who had, in days gone by, entertained Robert Moffat and visited his dwelling.

At this moment a waggon was seen approaching, and fearing it might contain some one from Griqua Town, and seeing that a hostile movement was made towards it, Moffat turned to Jantye and said, "I shall not see your face till the wag-gon and its owners are safe on the station." He instantly ran off and brought the waggon through, when it was found to contain the Wesleyan missionaries Mr. and Mrs. Archbell from Platberg.

At last, after much hesitation, Paul himself came near. He could not look at Moffat, and kept his hat drawn down over his eyes. He told the missionary that he himself need have no fear, but that revenge should be had upon the Batlaping who were at Kuruman.

"I shall have their blood and their cattle too," said Paul, as his eyes glared with fury.

Long and patiently Moffat argued with him, showing him the enormity of his crimes. At last the victory was won. No shot was fired, and both the station and the Batlaping were saved. Turning to his men, and referring to some of the missionary's cattle which had been stolen, he cried, "Bring back those cows and sheep we took this morning."

It was done. Then he said, "I am going. There are the things of your people. Will Mynheer not shake hands with me for once?"

"Of course I will," said Moffat, "but let me see your face."

"That I will not, indeed," he replied, "I do not want to die yet. I can see your face through my hat."

The rude hand of war was henceforth stayed, and the land had peace for half-a-century, during which time great and happy changes took place at the Kuruman station.

CHAPTER VII
THE AWAKENING

The long delayed, and fervently prayed for time had come at last. For ten weary years these earnest and faithful missionaries had laboured without seeing any results. Now their hearts were to rejoice as they should witness the work of the Holy Spirit, and see those over whom they had so long mourned, brought to the Saviour, and out of heathen darkness into Gospel light.

"The wind bloweth where it listeth, and thou hearest the sound thereof, but canst not tell whence it cometh, and whither it goeth;" so was it with the awakening among the Bechwanas at the Kuruman. There seemed no apparent cause for the intensity of feeling that was now displayed by these people. Men, who had scorned the idea of shedding a tear, wept as their hearts were melted. The chapel became a place of weeping, and some, after gazing intently upon the preacher, fell down in hysterics. The little chapel became too small to hold the numbers who flocked to it, and with the voluntary aid of Aaron Josephs a new building, fifty-one feet long by sixteen wide, with clay walls and thatched roof, was erected to serve as a schoolhouse and place of worship, until the large stone church, which was to form the most prominent feature of the station, should be completed.

This temporary church was opened in May, 1829, and in the following month, after very careful examination, six candidates for baptism were selected from among the inquirers. Speaking of these converts Robert Moffat said, "It was truly gratifying to observe the simplicity of their faith, implicitly relying on the atonement of Christ, of which they appeared to have a very clear conception, considering the previous darkness of their minds on such subjects."

They were baptised on the first Sabbath in July, a large number of spectators from the neighbouring towns, and a party of Griquas, being present. In the evening the missionaries, the new disciples, and a Griqua, twelve in all, sat down to the Lord's table. In connection with this event an interesting anecdote is related showing the strong faith of Mary Moffat!

On one occasion, some time before this event, when all seemed dark, her friend Mrs. Greaves of Sheffield had written to Mary Moffat kindly inquiring if there was anything of use which she could send. The reply returned was, "Send us a communion service, we shall want it some day." Communication between the Kuruman and England was tardy then, and before an answer came to her letter the darkness increased, and the Bechwanas seemed as far from salvation as ever. On the day preceding the reception of the first converts into the Kuruman Church, a box arrived from England, which had been twelve months on the road, and in it were found the communion vessels that Mary Moffat had asked for more than two years before.

Great as was the change, the missionaries rejoiced with trembling. They knew that there were great prejudices to be overcome, and that the relation in which the Christians stood to their heathen neighbours would expose their faith to trial. But they prayed and believed that He who had begun the good work would carry it on.

The change of heart speedily produced a change in dress and habits. Those who had been baptised had previously procured decent raiment, and prepared it for the occasion with Mrs. Moffat's assistance. A sewing-school had hitherto been uncalled for, the women's work having been that of building houses, raising fences, and tilling the ground; now Mrs. Moffat met those who desired to learn as often as her strength would permit, and soon she had a motley group of pupils, very few of the whole party possessing either a frock or a gown. The scarcity of materials was a serious impediment to progress, but ornaments, which before the natives had held in high repute, were now parted with to purchase the skins of animals, which being prepared almost as soft as cloth were made into jackets, trousers, and gowns. When a visit was paid by a trader, British manufactures were eagerly bought.

In the progress of improvement some amusing incidents occurred. A man might be seen in a jacket with one sleeve, because the other was not yet finished; or others went about in duffel jackets with sleeves of cotton of various colours; gowns like Joseph's coat were worn, and dresses of such fantastic shapes, that to tell the fashion of the same would have been a puzzle.

To Mrs. Moffat general application was made both by males and females. One brought skins to be cut into dresses, another wanted a jacket, a third a pattern, while a fourth brought his jacket sewed upside down, and asked why it did not fit. Fat, which before they always considered was to be rubbed on their bodies or deposited in their stomachs, they now found useful in making candles to give light in their dwellings.

The prospects of the missionaries continued cheering, and the increased anxiety for instruction and growth in knowledge among the candidates greatly strengthened their hands. "I seek Jesus," one would say; a second, "I am feeling after God, I have been wandering, unconscious of my danger, among beasts of prey; the day has dawned, I see my danger." The missionaries were cautious men, and were slow to receive members into their little church, but the evidence was complete that numbers were saved.

The happy death of a native woman about this time afforded them much encouragement. When she knew her end was near, she said to those around, "I am going to die. Weep not because I am going to leave you, but weep for your sins and your souls. With me all is well, for do not suppose that I die like a beast, or that I shall sleep for ever in the grave. No! Jesus has died for my sins; He has said he will save me, I am going to be with Him." Thus one who a few months before was as ignorant as the cattle, departed with the full assurance of an eternal life beyond the grave.

Rumours had for some time past reached the Kuruman station of a strong and warlike people who dwelt to the eastward, spoke another language, and were strangers to the Bechwanas. In the latter portion of 1829, two envoys were specially sent from Moselekatse, the king of this people, the Matabele, to the mission station at Kuruman, to learn about the manners and teaching of the white men there.

These envoys, who were two of the king's head men, were entertained, the principal objects, industries, and methods of living were pointed out to them; but their greatest wonder was excited when they beheld the public worship in the mission chapel. They listened to the hymns, and to the address, part of which only they understood, and were much surprised when they heard that the hymns were not war songs.

When the time came for the ambassadors to depart, they begged Robert Moffat to accompany them, as they were afraid of the Bechwana tribes through whom they would have to pass on their return journey. This circumstance led to his visiting the warlike Moselekatse, over whom he obtained a marvellous influence.

The details of the journey we must pass over. As they advanced they saw evidences on every hand of the terrible Mantatees, and the still more terrible Matabele. In places, where populous towns and villages had been, nothing remained but dilapidated walls and heaps of stones, mingled with human skulls. The country had become the abode of reptiles and beasts of prey; the inhabitants having perished beneath the spears and clubs of their savage enemies.

The reception accorded Robert Moffat by Moselekatse may best be described in the missionary's own words:—

"We proceeded directly to the town, and on riding into the centre of the large fold, we were rather taken by surprise to find it lined by eight hundred warriors, besides two hundred who were concealed on each side of the entrance, as if in ambush. We were beckoned to dismount, which we did, holding our horses' bridles in our hands. The warriors at the gate instantly rushed in with hideous yells, and leaping from the earth with a kind of kilt round their bodies, hanging like loose tails, and their large shields, frightened our horses. They then joined the circle, falling into rank with as much order as if they had been accustomed to European tactics. Here we stood, surrounded by warriors, whose kilts were of ape skins, and their legs and arms adorned with the hair and tails of oxen, their shields reaching to their chins and their heads adorned with feathers.

"A profound silence followed for some ten minutes; then all commenced a war-song, stamping their feet in time with the music. No one approached, though every eye was fixed upon us. Then all was silent, and Moselekatse marched out from behind the lines with an interpreter, and with attendants following, bearing meat, beer, and other food. He gave us a hearty salutation and seemed overjoyed."

The waggons were objects that struck the dusky monarch with awe. He examined them minutely, especially the wheels; one point remained a mystery, how the iron tire surrounding the wheel came to be in one piece without end or joint. Umbate, the head-man, who had visited the mission station, explained what he had seen in the smith's shop there. "My eyes," said he, "saw that very hand," pointing to Moffat's hand, "cut these bars of iron, take a piece off one end, and then join them as you now see them." "Does he give medicine to the iron?" the monarch inquired. "No," said Umbate, "nothing is used but fire, a hammer, and a chisel."

This powerful chieftain was an absolute despot ruling over a tribe of fierce warriors, who knew no will but his. He was the terror of all the surrounding country, his smile was life, his frown scattered horror and death. Yet even in his savage breast there were chords that could be touched by kindness, and Moffat received many tokens of his friendship during the eight days that he stayed in his town.

During one of their first interviews the monarch, laying his hand upon Moffats shoulder, said, "My heart is all white as milk; I am still wondering at the love of a stranger who never saw me. You have fed me, you have protected me, you have carried me in your arms. I live to-day by you, a stranger."

Upon Moffat replying that he was unaware of having rendered him any such service, he said, pointing to his two ambassadors: "These are great men; Umbate is my right hand. When I sent them from my presence to see the land of the white men, I sent my ears, my eyes, my mouth; what they heard I heard, what they saw I saw, and what they said it was Moselekatse who said it. You fed them and clothed them, and when they were to be slain you were their shield. You did it unto me. You did it unto Moselekatse, the son of Machobane."

Moffat explained to this African king the objects of the missionary, and pressed upon him the truths of the Gospel. On one occasion the king came attended by a party of his warriors, who remained at a short distance dancing and singing. "Their yells and shouts," says Moffat, "their fantastic leaps and distorted gestures, would have impressed a stranger with the idea that they were more like a company of fiends than men." As he looked upon the scene, his mind was occupied in contemplating the miseries of the savage state. He spoke to the king on man's ruin and man's redemption. "Why," said the monarch, "are you so earnest that I abandon all war, and do not kill men?" "Look on the human bones which lie scattered over your dominions," was the missionary's answer. "They speak in awful language, and to me they say, 'Whosoever sheddeth man's blood, by man also will his blood be shed.'" Moffat also spoke of the Resurrection, a startling subject for a savage and murderer like Moselekatse.

The kindness of the king extended to the missionary's return journey. Food in abundance was given to him, and a number of warriors attended his waggon as a guard against lions on the way. After an absence of two months he reached home in safety, where he found all well, and the Divine blessing still resting upon the Mission. Copious showers had fallen, and the fields and gardens teemed with plenty. The converts and many others, leaving their old traditions as to horticulture, imitated the example of the missionaries in leading out water to their gardens, and raised crops, not only of their native grain, pumpkins, kidney-beans, and water-melons, but also vegetables, such as the missionaries had introduced, maize, wheat, barley, peas, potatoes, carrots, onions, and tobacco—this latter they had formerly purchased from the Bahurutsi, but now it became a profitable article of traffic. They also planted fruit trees.

As an illustration of their zeal, which was not always according to knowledge, the following may be given. The course of the missionary's water-trench along the side of a hill, appeared as if it ascended, therefore several of the natives set to work in good earnest, and cut courses leading directly up hill, hoping the water would one day follow.

The spiritual affairs of the station kept pace with the external improvements. The temporary chapel continued to be well filled, a growing seriousness was observable among the people, progress was made in reading, and there was every reason for encouragement. Early In 1830, after the second mission-house had been finished and occupied by Mr. Hamilton, the foundation of a new and substantial stone church was laid. Circumstances, however, and especially the difficulty of procuring suitable timber for the roof delayed its completion for several years.

The work of translation had been kept steadily in view. In June, 1830, Robert Moffat had finished the translation into Sechwana, of the Gospel of Luke, and a long projected journey to the coast was undertaken by him and his wife. The journey had for its objects, to put the two elder children to school, to get the translation of Luke printed, and to collect subscriptions among friends in the Colony towards the building of the new place of worship.

At Philippolis, on their journey, they met with the French missionaries Rolland and Lemue, of the Paris Protestant Missionary Society, and also with Mr. and Mrs. Baillie, who had been appointed by the London Missionary Society to the Kururnan Mission. At Graham's Town, Mary Moffat remained behind to place the children at the Wesleyan school near there, and Robert visited several of the mission stations in Kafirland, and afterwards some of those within the Colony, finally reaching Cape Town in October, 1830.

At that early day printing in Cape Town was in its infancy. It was therefore found necessary to make application to the Governor to allow the Gospel of Luke In Sechwana to be printed at the Government Printing Office. The request was cheerfully acceded to, but compositors there were none to undertake the work. This difficulty, combined with the promise of an excellent printing press, which Dr. Philip had in his possession for the Kuruman Mission, induced Moffat to learn printing. He was joined by Mr. Edwards, who was now appointed to the Kuruman station, and under the kind superintendence of the assistant in charge of the office, they soon not only completed the work they had in hand, but acquired a fair knowledge of the art of printing. Besides the Gospel of Luke, a small hymn-book was printed in the Sechwana language.

A violent attack of bilious fever followed these labours, which had been carried on in the hottest season of the year, and when the time came for Robert Moffat to leave Cape Town he had to be carried on board the ship on a mattress. The sea passage to Algoa Bay, however, although a rough one, tended greatly to his restoration to health.

Sickness among their oxen, and the birth of a daughter, whom they named Elizabeth, detained the Moffats some time at Bethelsdorp, on their return journey; from which place, accompanied by Mr. and Mrs. Edwards, they went forward to the Kuruman, where they arrived in June, 1831. They carried with them the edition of the Gospel of Luke, a hymn-book printed in the language of the people, a printing-press, type, paper, and ink, besides liberal subscriptions from friends in the Colony towards the erection of the mission church.

Great was the astonishment of the natives when they saw the printing-press at work. Lessons, spelling-books and catechisms were prepared for the schools. To see a white sheet of paper disappear for a moment and then emerge covered with letters was beyond their comprehension. After a few noisy exclamations one obtained a sheet, with which he bounded through the village, showing it to all he met, and saying it had been made in a moment with a round black hammer (a printer's ball) and a shake of the arm.

A large box containing materials for clothing from a friend in Manchester, Miss

Lees, had also formed part of the baggage brought from the Cape. Materials being now at hand, and Mrs. Edwards and Mrs. Baillie co-operating, a sewing-school on a much larger scale was established, to the great comfort and improvement of the natives.

The congregation continued to increase and new members were added to the church, but sorrows tempered the joy of this happy time. Small-pox entered the country, and many of the inhabitants died; with them passed away one of the daughters of Robert and Mary Moffat. Towards the end of 1832 the labourers at Kuruman were cheered by a visit from Dr. Philip, who arranged that the two French missionaries, Rolland and Lemue, should commence a mission station at Motito, a place nearly forty miles distant, in a north-easterly direction.

In January, 1835, a scientific expedition under Dr. Andrew Smith, arrived at Moffat's station. This visit appeared as though ordered by an over-ruling Providence for the especial benefit of himself and his devoted wife. It found them in sore trouble, and it brought help and a friend in time of need. Mr. Edwards was away and Robert had been overworked. When Dr. Smith arrived, he found him suffering from an attack of intermittent fever, and hastened to render aid. Under the Doctor's skilful treatment he speedily recovered. On the 10th of March another son was added to the Moffat family, and shortly afterwards Mary was suddenly taken seriously ill, and became so weak, that for many days her recovery seemed hopeless. The Doctor was at that time away surveying, but upon receiving information of the position of affairs at Kuruman, he immediately hastened to render all the assistance in his power.

Speaking of this friend, raised up so unexpectedly, Robert Moffat writes in his book: "His tender sympathy and unremitting attention in that trying season, during which all hope of her recovery had fled, can never be erased from our grateful recollection, for in the midst of his active and laborious engagements at the head of the expedition, he watched for several successive nights, with fraternal sympathy, what appeared to be the dying pillow of my beloved partner, nor did he leave before she was out of danger."

A life-long friendship was cherished for the one who had come to them in their sore need, and who was always most gratefully remembered by the African missionary and his exemplary wife.

Shortly after these events, at the request of Dr. Smith, Robert Moffat accompanied the expedition on a visit to Moselekatse and the Matabele country. Moselekatse was delighted to see his missionary friend again. The scientific expedition had permission to travel through any part of the monarch's territories, but Moffat, the king kept as his guest. Together they visited, in the missionary's waggon, several of the Matabele towns, and many conversations were held, in which the importance of religion, and the evil effects of the king's policy were faithfully pointed out.

By this journey, which occupied three months, a way was paved for some American missionaries to reside with Moselekatse, and the country was surveyed to find timber suitable for the roof of the new Kuruman church. This timber was afterwards collected by Messrs. Hamilton and Edwards—the wood-cutters having to travel to a distance of two hundred and fifty miles—and fashioned into the roof of the church; which stands at this day a monument of the united labours of Hamilton, Moffat, and Edwards; and a wonder to beholders as to how such an achievement could have been performed with the slender means then at hand.

Upon Moffat's return home again, his wife, by Dr. Smith's orders, left for the Cape to recruit her strength; and Robert Moffat went itinerating among the scattered Bechwanas. A most interesting time was spent at a village, one hundred and fifty miles from Kuruman, where a chief named Mosheu and his people resided. Three times did the missionary preach to them on the first day, besides answering the questions of all who gathered round. Many were most anxious to learn to read, and such spelling-books as Moffat had with him were distributed among them.

Some of the head men thought they would like to try, and requested Moffat to teach them. A large sheet alphabet, torn at one corner, was found, and laid on the ground. All knelt in a circle round it, some of course viewing the letters upside down. "I commenced pointing with a stick," says he, "and when I pronounced one letter, all hallooed to some purpose. When I remarked that perhaps we might manage with somewhat less noise, one replied, 'that he was sure the louder he roared, the sooner would his tongue get accustomed to the seeds' as he called the letters."

Somewhat later, a party of young folks seized hold of the missionary, with the request, "Oh, teach us the A B C with music." Dragged and pushed, he entered one of the largest native houses, which was instantly crowded. The tune of "Auld Lang Syne" was pitched to A B C, and soon the strains were echoed to the farthest

MOFFAT PREACHING AT MOSHEU'S VILLAGE.

corner of the village. Between two and three o'clock on the following morning, Moffat got permission to retire to rest; his slumbers were, however, disturbed by the assiduity of the sable choristers; and on awaking after a brief repose, his ears were greeted on all sides by the familiar notes of the Scotch air.

Very pleasing progress was made by these people in Christian knowledge. Mosheu brought his daughter to Mrs. Moffat for instruction, and his brother took his son to Mr. Lemue at Motito for the same purpose.

The mission at the Kuruman continued to prosper, both at the home and the out-stations. Numbers of Bechwanas were added to the church, both at Kuruman and Griqua Town. Under Mr. Edwards' superintendence the readers largely increased, and the Infant School, commenced and carried on by Mrs. Edwards, with the assistance of a native girl, was highly satisfactory. Civilisation advanced, some of the natives purchasing waggons, and using oxen for labour which formerly had been performed by women. Clothing was in such demand, that a merchant named Hume, an honourable trader in whom the missionaries had confidence, built a house, and settled at the station. The new church, after much labour, was opened in November, 1838, on which occasion between eight and nine hundred persons attended the service; and on the following Sabbath, one hundred and fifty members united in celebrating the Lord's Supper.

Persevering Christian love, combined with strong faith, much prayer, and untiring labour, had changed the barren wilderness into a fruitful land.

CHAPTER VIII
VISIT TO ENGLAND

The work of Bible translation had been steadily pressed forward; all available time having been devoted by Robert Moffat to that undertaking. By the end of 1838, the whole of the New Testament had been rendered into the native tongue, and a journey was made by the Moffats to Cape Town, to recruit their health, and to get the Sechwana New Testament printed; the task being too heavy for the mission press. Cape Town was but little better off than the Kuruman for accomplishing a work of this magnitude, and it speedily became apparent that the printing would have to be undertaken in England.

Twenty-two years had passed away since the youthful missionary stood upon the deck of the *Alacrity*, and bade farewell to the land of his birth. During that time he had never allowed his interest in the affairs of his native country to grow cold. Letters and newspapers had been eagerly welcomed, and the memory of friends in the far distant isle had been most keenly cherished, both by him and his Mary. Now once more they were to tread upon its well-loved shores, and to tell to its people the story of God's work among the savage tribes of South Africa.

There were no floating "Castles"[1] at that time, making the journey in twenty days, and a passage had to be taken in a small ship homeward-bound from China, having troops on board. Measles raged at the Cape, and sickness was on board ship. Between the two the Moffats had much to endure, and the vessel had not left Table Bay when another daughter was born to add to their joy and anxiety. Three days' after his sister came, dear six-year-old Jamie, lying beside his prostrate mother in her cot, was called to the Better Land, with the words, "Oh, that will be joyful,

1 Donald Currie's line of Mail steamships, the *Garth Castle*, &c., which make the voyage to the Cape in twenty days.

when we meet to part no more," upon his dying lips.

On the 6th June, 1839, the ship anchored off Cowes, and a few days later reached London. The reception of Robert Moffat was most enthusiastic, and so great was the demand for his presence at public meetings, that it was with the utmost difficulty he procured liberty to visit his own friends.

Twenty years had made great changes in the homes at both Dukinfield and Inverkeithing. Mary Moffat's aged father was living, but her mother and a brother had been called away, another brother was in America, and a third was a missionary in Madras. Robert's parents were still living, but a brother and two sisters had passed away. Many friends, whose kind and generous thoughtfulness had often cheered the heart of the faithful missionary and his faithful wife in their voluntary exile, now gathered around them, among whom were Mrs. Greaves of Sheffield, the donor of the Communion Service, and Miss Lees of Manchester.

Of the events connected with this visit to England, want of space precludes us from giving details. A great wave of missionary enthusiasm at that time swept over the country, and Moffat found himself hurried from town to town with but scant opportunities for rest. In May, 1840, he preached the Anniversary Sermon for the London Missionary Society, and, at their Annual Meeting, Exeter Hall was packed so densely that after making his speech in the large upper hall, Moffat had to give it again in the smaller hall below.

An anecdote related in the course of his speech at the Bible Society's May Meeting shows the value set by a native woman upon a single Gospel in the native tongue. "She was a Matabele captive," said Moffat. "Once, while visiting the sick, as I entered her premises, I found her sitting weeping, with a portion of the Word of God in her hand. I said, 'My child what is the cause of your sorrow? Is the baby still unwell?' 'No,' she replied, 'my baby is well,' 'Your mother-in-law?' I inquired. 'No, no,' she said, 'it is my own dear mother, who bore me.' Here she again gave vent to her grief, and, holding out the Gospel of Luke, in a hand wet with tears, she said, 'My mother will never see this word; she will never hear this good news! Oh, my mother and my friends, they live in heathen darkness; and shall they die without seeing the light which has shone on me, and without tasting that love which I have tasted!' Raising her eyes to heaven she sighed a prayer, and I heard the words again, 'My mother, my mother!'"

His hope when he landed had been to get the printing of the Sechwana New Testament speedily accomplished, and to return to South Africa before winter; but it was not until January, 1843, that he was able once again to sail for Africa.

In 1840 two new missionaries were set apart for the Bechwana mission—William Ross and David Livingstone. With them Robert Moffat was able to send five hundred copies of the Sechwana New Testament.

As the sheets were passing through the press, it was suggested to him that the Psalms would be a valuable addition to the work. With his characteristic energy he immediately commenced the task, and, a few months after the sailing of Ross and Livingstone, he had the joy of sending to Africa over two thousand copies of the New Testament, with which the Psalms had been bound up. By the end of 1843 six thousand copies had been sent out. A revision of the book of Scripture Lessons was also undertaken and carried through the press. A demand was made upon him to write a book, in response to which he prepared his well known work, "Missionary Labours and Scenes in South Africa," which was published in 1842, and met with great success.

At length the time drew near when once more Robert and Mary Moffat should cross the sea to their beloved home at Kuruman. Valedictory services of a most enthusiastic character were held in Scotland, Newcastle, Manchester, and London. At Edinburgh a copy of the "Encyclopaedia Britannica" was presented to Robert Moffat, and at Newcastle a set of scientific instruments was given him. A great impetus was imparted to missionary work abroad through these and preceding meetings, during his sojourn in England, and when on the 30th of January, 1843, he and his wife embarked at Gravesend, accompanied by two new missionaries for the Bechwana field, they carried with them the esteem of a wide circle of friends, and had the fervent prayers of many offered up on their behalf.

On the 10th of April they landed at Cape Town, and six weeks later embarked in a small coasting vessel for Algoa Bay. At Bethelsdorp, a village a few miles beyond Port Elizabeth, they rejoined Messrs. Ashton and Inglis, who with their wives had gone on before by steamer; but here they were detained for several months, waiting for a vessel to arrive from England which had on board a large quantity of baggage for the missionaries and their work.

CAPE TOWN.

At last the start was made, the long train of ox waggons wended their way, the Orange River was crossed, this time on a pont or floating bridge, and at the Vaal River, one hundred and fifty miles distant from Kuruman, the missionary party were met by David Livingstone, who had ridden forth to bid them welcome.

From this point onwards friends both white and black emulated each other in testifying their gladness at their friend's return, until as the Moffats drew near to Kuruman their progress became like a royal one. At last between two and three o'clock on the 10th of December, 1843, they sat down once again in their own home, amongst those for whom they had toiled so zealously, and over whom their hearts yearned with a holy love. The delight of the natives at having their missionary and his wife among them again was unbounded. In a letter published in the *Missionary Magazine*, October, 1844, Moffat thus writes, giving an account of their reception:—"Many were the hearty welcomes we received, all appearing emulous to testify their joy. Old and young, even the little children, would shake hands with us. Some gave vent to their joy with an air of heathen wildness, and some in silent floods of tears; while others, whose hearts had sickened with deferred hope, would ask again and again, 'Do our eyes indeed behold you?' Thus we found ourselves once more among a people who loved us, and who had longed for our return."

The mission having been largely reinforced, it was arranged that Mr, and Mrs. Ross should go to Taung, about one hundred miles east of Kuruman, where a portion of the Bechwana tribe had settled under Mahura, a brother of Mothibi; while Edwards and Livingstone were to commence work among the Bakhatla, two hundred miles to the north-east. Inglis was to go to the same neighbourhood; thus the regular missionary staff of the Kuruman station comprised after their departure, the venerable Mr. Hamilton, who had seen the commencement of the Bechwana Mission in 1816, Mr. and Mrs. Ashton, and the Moffats.

The place to which Edwards and Livingstone had gone was a large native town near to the haunts of lions. These greatly harassed the cattle and deprived the missionaries of sleep. One day a hunt was arranged. Livingstone joined the party, was attacked by the lion, and was only rescued with a broken and mangled arm by the bravery and devotion of his native servant, Mebalwe, who himself got severely bitten.

LIVINGSTONE ATTACKED BY A LION.

During his recovery from this injury Livingstone visited the Kuruman, and there won the heart of Moffat's eldest daughter, her mother's namesake, who soon afterwards exchanged the name of Mary Moffat for that of Mary Livingstone. In due course she accompanied her husband to Chonwane where for a time he was located with Sechele, the chief of the Bakwena.

The life of the missionaries at the Kuruman was a, busy one. All were fully employed. Moffat's principal work was translation, and in this his colleague Ashton afforded him much critical assistance, besides relieving him almost entirely of the duties of the printing office. But other work had to be undertaken. The natives needed much help and guidance; dwelling-houses had to be enlarged and new schoolrooms built, and, as there were no funds for the payment of artisans, the missionaries had to put their own hands to the work; besides which, as money was not forthcoming to meet the cost of the new schoolrooms, a kind of amateur store was opened by the missionaries' wives for the sale of clothing to the natives.

The Rev. J. J. Freeman who visited Africa a few years later, in 1849, gives us a picture of the Kuruman station as he saw it. "It wears," says he, "a very pleasing appearance. The mission premises, with the walled gardens opposite, form a street wide and long. The chapel is a substantial and well-looking building of stone. By the side of it stands Mr. Moffat's house, simple yet commodious. In a cottage hard by, the venerable Hamilton was passing his declining days, extremely feeble, but solaced by the motherly care of his colleague's wife. The gardens were well stocked with fruit and vegetables, requiring much water, but easily getting it from the 'fountain.' On the Sunday morning the chapel bell rang for early service. Breakfasting at seven, all were ready for the schools at half-past eight. The infants were taught by Miss Moffat (their daughter Ann, afterwards Mrs. Fredoux) in their school-house; more advanced classes were grouped in the open air, or collected in the adjacent buildings. Before ten the work of separate teaching ceased, and young and old assembled for public worship. A sanctuary, spacious and lofty, and airy withal, was comfortably filled with men, women, and children, for the most part decently dressed."

This description may be supplemented by that of a scene of frequent occurrence, given in "Robert and Mary Moffat" by their son Mr. John A. Moffat. He says: "The public services were, of course, in the Sechwana language. Once a week the missionary families met for an English devotional meeting. It was also a sort of custom that as the sun went down there should be a short truce from work every evening. A certain eminence at the back of the station became, by common consent, the meeting-place. There the missionary fathers of the hamlet would be found, each sitting on his accustomed stone. Before them lay the broad valley, once a reedy morass, now reclaimed and partitioned out into garden lands; its margin fringed with long water-courses, overhung with grey willows and the dark green syringa. On the low ground bordering the valley stood the church, with its attendant mission-houses and schools, and on the heights were perched the native villages, for the most part composed of round, conical huts, not unlike corn-stacks at a distance, with some more ambitious attempts at house-building in the shape of semi-European cottages. Eastward stretched a grassy plain, bounded by the horizon, and westward a similar plain, across which about five miles distant, was a range of low hills. Down to the right, in a bushy dell, was the little burying-ground, marked by a few trees."

In 1845, Robert Moffat narrowly escaped an accident that would have involved most serious consequences. He was superintending the erection of a new corn-mill, and whilst seeing to its being properly started, incautiously stretched his arm over two cog-wheels. In an instant the shirt sleeve was caught and drawn in, and with it the arm. Fortunately the mill was stopped in time, but an ugly wound, six inches in length, with torn edges, bore witness to the danger escaped. This wound laid him aside for many weeks, but finally he recovered from the effects of the accident.

For the next four or five years things pursued an even course at the Kuruman. In 1846, Mary Moffat started on a journey to visit the Livingstones at Chonwane. She availed herself of the escort of a native hunting party, and took her three younger children with her. She passed through the usual dangers of such a journey, as the following extract from a letter written to her husband will show:—

"I am very glad of Boey's company.... I should indeed have felt very solitary with my lone waggon with ignorant people, but he is so completely at home in this field that one feels quite easy. We do not stop at nights by the waters, but come to them at mid-day, and then leave about three or four o'clock. We cannot but be constantly on the outlook for lions, as we come on their spoor every day, and the people sometimes hear them roar. Just before outspanning to-day, Boey, being on horseback looking for water, met with a majestic one, which stood still and looked at him. He tried to frighten the lion, but he stood his ground, when Boey thought it was time to send a ball into him, which broke his leg, by which means he is disabled from paying us a visit."

Early in 1847 a general meeting of those engaged in the Bechwana mission was held at Lekatlong (near what are now the Diamond Fields). On his way homewards from this meeting Moffat visited some of the Batlaping villages along the Kolong River. A striking advance had taken place of late years, and a severe contest was going on between heathenism and Christianity. A little company of believers had gathered in each place, and were ministered to by native teachers, who had spent a few months in training at Kuruman.

In the same year Mary Moffat left for the Cape to make arrangements for educating her younger children. As Robert could not leave his work she journeyed alone, having as attendants four Bechwana men and a maid. These partings wrung the mother's heart. The time spent on the road was precious, and although it extended to two months, seemed all too short. She felt that never again would she have her young children about her. The son, John, was placed at school in Cape Town for a time, and the two daughters were sent under the care of a worthy minister to England. Of the parting with these her darlings Mary Moffat wrote:—"Though my heart was heaving with anguish I joyfully and thankfully acceded forthwith (*i.e.*, to the offer of the Rev. J. Crombie Brown to take the children), and set about preparations in good earnest. This was about the end of January. On the tenth of February they embarked, and after stopping the night on board I tore myself from my darlings to return to my desolate lodgings to contemplate my solitary journey, and to go to my husband and home childless." Of her it may be said, *She left all and followed Him*!

In 1848 the book of Proverbs and Ecclesiastes had been finished and Isaiah begun. In 1849 "Pilgrim's Progress" was added to the Sechwana literature, and the work of translation steadily progressed. "Line upon Line" had also been rendered into the native tongue by Mr. Ashton.

But while all was peaceful and in a measure prosperous at the Kuruman, clouds were gathering to the eastward, which were destined eventually to throw a dark shadow over the whole Bechwana Mission. The encroachments of the Boers upon the natives led to much bloodshed, and to the dispersion of several native tribes, with the consequent abandonment of mission-work among them. One of the early sufferers was Moselekatse, who, having been attacked in 1837, had retired to a place far away to the north-east, and for some years nothing was heard of him, except by vague rumour; indeed his very existence was a matter of doubt.

Livingstone had settled with Sechele at Kolobeng, which place he used simply as a base of operations for visiting the eastern tribes, and prosecuting missionary work among them. Much good was done, and the Scriptures in Sechwana, as far as issued, were circulated among the people. But the Boers advanced, the natives were dispossessed of their lands, and missionaries were expelled from their regions. Finding that all hope of carrying on the work in this neighbourhood was over,

Livingstone turned his eyes northward, and commenced that series of explorations which absorbed the remainder of his life. Sechele retired to a mountain fastness, named Lithubaruba, away to the north-west.

As time passed onward, Robert Moffat felt more than ever the importance of completing the work he had undertaken—the translation of the entire Bible into Sechwana. Every minute that could be devoted to the task was eagerly embraced, his labours often extending far into the night. Numerous interruptions made the work more difficult. "Many, many are the times I have sat down and got my thoughts somewhat in order," he writes, "with pen in hand to write a verse, the correct rendering of which I had just arrived at, after wading through other translations and lexicons, when one enters my study with some complaint he has to make, or counsel to ask, or medical advice and medicine to boot, a tooth to be extracted, a subscription to the auxiliary to be measured or counted; or one calls to say he is going to the Colony, and wishes something like a passport; anon strangers from other towns, and visitors from the interior arrive, who all seem to claim a right to my attentions."

This incessant application was making inroads upon his health, and the strong powerful frame and iron constitution of the Scotch missionary began to show signs that could not be neglected. A peculiar affection of the head troubled him—a constant roaring noise like the falling of a cataract, and a buzzing as of a boiling up of waters. It never ceased day and night, and he lost much sleep in consequence of it. His only relief seemed to be in study and preaching, when the malady was not noticed; but immediately these occupations were over it was found to be there, and reasserted itself in full force.

In 1851 the rebellion of the Kat River Hottentots occurred, which, for a long time, brought obloquy upon the missionaries of South Africa and the Mission cause.

In 1852 Mr. Hamilton was gathered to his rest, after having been the faithful coadjutor of Robert Moffat, and a missionary at the Kuruman for thirty-four years; the next year tidings reached Mary Moffat that her beloved father had ended his pilgrimage at the ripe age of ninety years.

A short time previous a letter had been received from the Directors of the London Missionary Society, urging Robert Moffat to take sick leave and visit the

Cape, or to return to England, but, as rest and change were absolutely essential, Moffat determined to find the needed relaxation in visiting his old native friend, Moselekatse. He was also in doubt as to the fate of his son-in-law, Livingstone, who had started long before for the tribes on the Zambesi.

Carrying supplies for that missionary, in hope of being able to succour him, in May, 1854, Moffat once again bade his faithful partner farewell, and started for a journey to a comparatively unknown country, seven or eight hundred miles away. The son of Mr. Edwards, the missionary who for some time had laboured with Moffat at Kuruman, and a young man named James Chapman accompanied him, for purposes of trade. After journeying for several days through a desert country, they reached Sechele's mountain fastness. Moffat found that chief in great difficulties, but still holding to the faith into which he had been baptised by Livingstone. One hundred and twenty more miles of desert travelling brought the party to Shoshong, the residence of another chief and his tribe. Thence after groping their way for eighteen days in a region new to them, without guides, they reached a village containing some natives who were subject to the Matabele king.

For some days Moffat and his companions were not allowed to advance. The Induna in charge of the outpost was afraid of a mistake, but at last a message came that they were to proceed, and finally they drew near to the royal abode. The chief was filled with joy at meeting his old friend "Moshete." An account of the interview is described in Moffat's journal, from which we extract the following:—"On turning round, there he sat—how changed! The vigorous, active, and nimble chief of the Matabele, now aged, sitting on a skin, lame in his feet, unable to walk, or even to stand. I entered, he grasped my hand, gave one earnest look, and drew his mantle over his face. It would have been an awful sight for his people to see the hero of a hundred fights wipe from his eyes the falling tears. He spoke not, except to pronounce my name, Moshete, again and again. He looked at me again, his hand still holding mine, and he again covered his face. My heart yearned with compassion for his soul. Drawing a little nearer to the outside, so as to be within sight of Mokumbate, his venerable counsellor, he poured out his joy to him."

The old chief was suffering with dropsy, but under Moffat's medical care he recovered, and was soon able to walk about again. The advice which had been given to him by his missionary friend during their previous intercourse, had not been wholly lost, the officers who attended him, as well as those of lower grades, stating that the rigour of his government had since that time been greatly modified.

Moffat stayed with Moselekatse nearly three months. After much persuasion, permission was given him to preach the Gospel to the Matabele people, a privilege hitherto always denied. On the 24th of September, 1854, these people received, for the first time, instruction in the subjects of creation, providence, death, redemption, and immortality.

It was Moffat's purpose to journey forward beyond the Matabele to the Makololo tribe, to leave supplies at their town of Linyanti, so that Livingstone might obtain them if he returned safely from St. Paul de Loanda, on the west coast. Moselekatse would not accede to the idea of him going alone, and finally the king himself determined to accompany him. The Makololo and Matabele were, however, like many other of the native tribes, hostile to each other. With the bags, boxes, &c., on the heads of some of the men best acquainted with the country, the party set out, but after travelling to the farthest outpost of the Marabele, the king declared it was impossible for the waggons to proceed. At Moffat's earnest request, he sent forward a party of his men with the supplies, which in due course reached the Makololo, who placed them on an island, built a roof over them, and there they were found in safety by Livingstone when he returned some months afterwards from the west coast.

Towards the end of October, Moffat bade farewell to the Matabele king. Moselekatse pressed him to prolong his stay, pleading that he had not seen enough of him, and that he had not yet shown him sufficient kindness. "Kindness!" replied Moffat, "you have overwhelmed me with kindness, and I shall now return with a heart overflowing with thanks." Leaving the monarch a supply of suitable medicines to keep his system in tolerable order, and admonishing him to give up beer drinking, and to receive any Christian teacher who might come as he had received him, the missionary took his departure. The long return journey was accomplished without any remarkable event, and in due course Moffat reached his home again in safety.

By this journey his health was much improved, his intercourse and friendship with the people of the interior were cemented and extended, and he looked forward with hopeful assurance to the early advancement of Christianity to those distant regions.

CHAPTER IX
THE SECHWANA BIBLE

The great task was at length accomplished; the work of nearly thirty years brought to a close. The Word of God in the language of the Bechwana people, in all its glorious completeness and power, was now in their hands.

To Robert Moffat the labour had been of a herculean character. He had spared himself no labour or drudgery which its prosecution involved. To accomplish it he had left his home and lived a semi-savage life for nearly three months, that he might perfect himself in the language. Without any special training for the important undertaking, and under the greatest disadvantages, he had not only acquired the language, but reduced it to its elements, and then presented it in a synthetic and grammatical form. Beyond that his earnest desire had been to render the whole Bible into the native tongue.

As age increased, the importance of finishing the work became more and more apparent, till even a minute spent in anything but purely mission-work, or his translation duties, seemed as wasted time. Writing when the end was near, he said: "When I take up a newspaper, it is only to glance at it with a feeling like that of committing sacrilege. I have sometimes been arrested with something interesting, and have read it with ten or more strokes in the minute added to my pulse, from the anxiety caused by the conviction that I am spending precious time apart from its paramount object, while I feel perfectly composed over anything which I am satisfied has a direct bearing on the true object of the missionary."

But the work was now accomplished, the last sheet had been passed for press, the last verse of the Old Testament completed, and now his mind, which had been for so many years strained under the weighty responsibility of translating the Word of God, was free. Of his feelings on this occasion he made mention in a speech delivered some years later at Port Elizabeth, on the occasion of his final departure from South Africa. We quote from the Chronicle of the London Missionary Society for August, 1870.

"At last," he said, referring to the commencement of the undertaking, "I came to the resolution that if no one else would do it, I would undertake it myself. I entered heartily upon the work. For many years I had no leisure, every spare moment being devoted to translating, and was a stranger even in my own family. There was labour every day, for back, for hands, for head. This was especially the case during the time Mr. Edwards was there; our condition was almost one of slavery. Still the work advanced, and at last I had the satisfaction of completing the New Testament. Of this 6000 copies were printed by the Home Society.

"When Dr. Livingstone came, he urged me to begin at once with the Old Testament. That was a most stupendous work. Before commencing it I passed many sleepless nights. It was the wish of all that I should undertake it. I did so, and went on with the work from time to time, as I had leisure, daily and nightly. I stuck to it till I had got as far as the end of Kings, when I became completely done up. The Directors were afraid that I was killing myself. I was advised to go home, to leave the work, but I decided otherwise. I determined to look up Moselekatse, and went off with a son of brother Edwards. By the time I had found Moselekatse, I had got all right again. I came back and resumed my work, and continued it till its completion. I cannot describe to you the feelings of that time—of the writing of the last verse. I could hardly believe that I was in the world, so difficult was it for me to realise the fact that my labour of years was completed. Whether it was from weakness or overstrained mental exertion, I cannot tell; but a feeling came over me that I would die, and I felt perfectly resigned. To overcome this I went back again to my manuscript still to be printed, read it over, and re-examined it, till at length I got back again to my right mind. This was the most remarkable time of my life, a period I shall never forget. My feelings found vent by my falling upon my knees and thanking God for His grace and goodness in giving me strength to accomplish my task. My work was thus accomplished, and now I see the Word of God read by thousands of Bechwanas in their native tongue."

DR. LIVINGSTONE.

An incident related in his speech at the Bible Society's Annual Meeting upon the occasion of his first visit to England in 1839, shows the importance to the natives of having the Bible in their own tongue. Speaking of his translation of the Gospel of Luke, he alluded to the state of the unconverted heathen, and the contrast manifested by the Christian converts. When the heathen saw the converts reading the Book which had produced this change, they inquired if they (the converts) talked to it. "No," answered they, "it talks to us; for it is the Word of God." "What then," replied the strangers, "does it *speak*?" "Yes," said the Christians, "it speaks to the heart!" This explanation was true, and was often illustrated in fact; for among those to whom the same Book was read by others, it became proverbial to say that the readers were "turning their hearts inside out!"

In 1854 Mary Moffat paid another visit to the Colony, and was in consequence away from home when Robert returned from his journey to Moselekatse. Tidings reached him about that time of the death of his mother, the one who first instilled into his breast an enthusiasm for the missionary calling. She died as she had lived, a godly, consistent woman, and was called to the heavenly city at the age of eighty-four.

In 1856 Dr. Livingstone, after his unparalleled walk from Loanda, on the west coast, to Quillimane, on the east—from the shores of the Atlantic to those of the Indian Ocean—visited England. His visit, and the description he gave of the country and natives, rekindled missionary enthusiasm, a special interest being taken in the Matabele and Makololo tribes. The London Missionary Society resolved to establish missions among them. As the locality where the Makololo dwelt was in the midst of a marshy network of rivers, it was considered as a necessary condition of commencing the proposed missionary work that they should remove to a spot on the north bank of the Zambesi, opposite to where the Matabele dwelt on the south bank. The two tribes were, however, hostile to each other; and, to overcome this hostility, it was determined to simultaneously establish missions among both tribes. With this object in mind the Directors wrote to Robert Moffat, proposing that he should go for a twelvemonth to the Matabele, taking two younger men with him, and plant a mission among this people.

This letter reached him just as he had completed the translation and printing of the Old Testament; and, notwithstanding that he was then sixty-two years of age, and had already been forty-one years hard at work for the Society, he determined to go. He felt, however, that it was necessary for him to start at once, and prepare the minds of Moselekatse and his people for the coming among them of missionaries. Thus it came about that once again Robert Moffat quitted Kuruman, and started forward for the long and trying journey, through the African desert, to visit his old friend, and obtain his consent to the settlement of missionaries among his people.

Visiting the chief Sechele on the way, he pursued his course until he at length reached the headquarters of Moselekatse. The king was not very enthusiastic about receiving missionaries for himself and his people. He was somewhat suspicious; and his former experience with the American missionaries at Mosega had been rather unfortunate, the Boers having attacked the Matabele, and, after pillaging the mission station, carried the missionaries away with them. However, he would receive the new-comers,—but his friend Moshete must come also. "I love you," said he, "you are my father. These new men I do not know them. All men are not alike."

This African monarch had sufficient knowledge to know that, if the doctrines of the Bible prevailed among his tribe, his claims to divine honour would for ever cease. His warriors used to pay him homage as follows: "O Pezoolu, the king of kings, king of the heavens, who would not fear before the son of Machobane (his father's name), mighty in battle?" and with other similar marks of adulation. He also had a shrewd suspicion that the opening of the country for white men to come and settle, would mean, eventually, the downfall of the power of himself and his people? but in his friend Ramary, or Moshete, he had implicit confidence.

As an instance of the power which Moffat had obtained over this despotic chief of a fierce African tribe, it may be related that he prevailed upon Moselekatse to grant deliverance to the heir to the chieftainship of the Bamangwato, a large tribe living at Shoshong, to the north-east of Sechele's people. It was after a long conversation that the thing was settled. Macheng, the heir, who had been detained captive for sixteen years, was called, and Moselekatse addressing him said: "Macheng, man of Moffat, go with your father. We have arranged respecting you. Moffat will take you back to Sechele. That is my wish as well as his, that you should be in the first instance restored to the chief from whom you were taken in war. When captured you were a child; I have reared you to be a man."

The effect of this deliverance on the neighbouring tribes was very great. It occurred while Moffat was with Moselekatse, arranging for the settlement of the new missionaries. When he and his charge arrived at Sechele's town, on his way home, he was met by Sechele and the other chiefs of his tribe, who marched on in front, and led them to a kind of natural amphitheatre, where at least ten thousand of the people, in all their equipments of war, were assembled. Sechele commanded silence, and introduced the business of the meeting. Speaker followed speaker, in enthusiastic language giving expression to the joy they felt at seeing the chief of the Bamangwato return from captivity. In the course of his speech one said as follows:—

"Ye tribes, ye children of the ancients, this day is a day of marvel.... Now I begin to perceive that those who preach are verily true. If Moffat were not of God, he would not have espoused the cause of Sechele, in receiving his words, and delivering Macheng from the dwelling-place of the beasts of prey, to which we Bechwanas dared not approach. There are those who contend that there is nothing in religion. Let such to-day throw away their unbelief. If Moffat were not such a man, he would not have done what he has done, in bringing him who was lost—him who was dead—from the strong bondage of the mighty. Moselekatse is a lion; he conquered nations, he robbed the strong ones, he bereaved mothers, he took away the son of Kheri. We talk of love. What is love? We hear of the love of God. Is it not through the love of God that Macheng is among us to-day? A stranger, one of a nation—who of you knows its distance from us?—he makes himself one of us, enters the lion's abode, and brings out to us our own blood."

On reaching home, from his visit to the Matabele, Moffat found that the Livingstones were starting for the Zambesi, and were to call at the Cape on their way; also that a large party of new missionaries had been appointed to commence the new interior missions. The Moffats at once started for the Cape, and there met Dr. and Mrs. Livingstone and their companions. Once more the mother and daughter embraced each other, and as the latter had suffered much on the voyage, it was arranged that she should accompany the missionary party, and travel overland to the Zambesi.

At Cape Town Moffat also had the pleasure of welcoming his own son, the Rev. John Moffat, who was to proceed to the Matabele as a missionary, paid for out of Dr. Livingstone's private resources. Sir George Grey, Her Majesty's High Commissioner, warmly encouraged the proposed plans for extending Christianity and commerce to the interior tribes, and arranged with Robert Moffat for establishing a postal communication with the Zambesi *via* Kuruman.

All arrangements having been completed the missionaries left Cape Town on their way to Kuruman, from whence they were to proceed to their respective stations, with the Makololo and the Matabele. Delays, however, intervened; the Boers had attacked some of the Batlapings, and threatened to attack the Kuruman station; the difficulties of the road also prevented some of the party arriving with the others. At last, however, the way was made clear, the opposition of the Boers to the advance of the party was, through the intervention of Sir George Grey, overcome, and on the 7th of July, 1859, the first division started for their far distant destination. This division comprised Mr. Helmore, a veteran who for many years had been stationed at Lekatlong, with his wife and four children, and Mr. and Mrs. Price. There was also a native teacher from Lekatlong, named Tabe, who determined to accompany his old missionary, and the usual staff of native attendants. These were all to proceed to the Makololo. The situation was a grave one. The end of the journey was a point a thousand miles farther into the interior than any of them had ever been, except two native servants, who had accompanied Livingstone on a previous occasion. But they went forward in faith not knowing what lay before them, but trusting all into the hands of Him, without whose knowledge not even a sparrow falls to the ground.

A week later Mr. Thomas and John Moffat with their wives left; they were speedily followed by Robert Moffat and Mr. Sykes. At Sechele's town the two portions of this latter division were united, and thence they journeyed onwards towards the Matabele. Disease broke out among some of their oxen, and, on reaching the first outpost of Moselekatse's people, a messenger was sent forward to the king explaining the state of affairs, and proposing that the oxen of the missionaries should be left in quarantine, and that Moselekatse should supply his own oxen to bring the party to headquarters. This message was sent so as to avoid connecting the advent of the Gospel among these people with that of a pestilence among their herds of cattle; which would inevitably have been the case had the diseased oxen proceeded onwards and infected those belonging to the Matabele.

An answer was returned to the effect that the party were to proceed, and that though the epidemic took effect, they should be held guiltless.

Moffat despatched a second messenger, to say that he had heard the king's words, and in a couple of days would leave; but that he begged the monarch to reflect on the consequences of the epidemic being introduced among his tens of thousands of cattle, and to believe that the mission party felt the most extreme anxiety upon the subject.

They then proceeded forward very slowly for two or three days, when they were met by another messenger, who stated that Moselekatse was gratified with the anxiety expressed for him and his; and that now, fully convinced of his danger, he desired that all their oxen should return, and that warriors were advancing to drag the mission waggons to headquarters.

Every one started with surprise at the strange idea, but soon the warriors came, shields, and spears, and all, also a number of oxen to be slaughtered for food. After some war evolutions, the warriors took the place of the draught oxen, and a start was made. There was many "a strong pull, a long pull, and a pull all together," as the waggons rolled onward; but after ten days' hard struggle and slow progress, it became evident that the men sent were unequal to the task, and the monarch, who for some unknown reason had kept his oxen back, sent them at last to bring the waggons to his camp.

Moselekatse received his old friend with his usual cordiality; but it soon became evident that something was wrong. All kinds of evasions and delays met the request for a spot of ground on which to found a mission station; days, weeks, and months passed, during which the missionaries suffered great hardships; and at last the chief broke up his camp and left them, without oxen to draw their waggons, saying that he would send people to guide them to the spot where they were to settle, and at which place he would join them later on.

His conduct seemed strange, and Moffat began to suspect that he had repented of giving his permission for the missionaries to settle with him. This proved to be the case; the Boer inroads, following as they had done, in several cases, the advent of the missionaries, made him suspicious, and the fears of himself and people having been aroused, the question was in debate as to whether the settlement should be allowed or not.

At last a favourable change took place, the clouds dispersed, and the sky became clear. Oxen were sent to take the missionary waggons forward to Inyati, there to join Moselekatse. All was settled, a spot which looked well for a station was pointed out, each of the new-comers pitched his tent under a tree that he had chosen, until a more solid dwelling should be erected, and the Matabele Mission was fairly established. This was in December, 1859.

The Mission was established, but work had only begun. The first six months of the year 1860 were months of incessant toil to the missionaries at Inyati. Houses had to be built, waggons repaired, and garden ground made ready for cultivation. Early and late, Moffat was to be found at work,—in the saw-pit, at the blacksmith's forge, or exercising his skill at the carpenter's bench; in all ways aiding and encouraging his younger companions. He also endeavoured to gain Moselekatse's consent to the opening of regular communication with the Livingstone expedition on the Zambesi *via* Matabeleland, but the suspicious nature of the monarch foiled this project. The isolation of his country in this direction was so great that, although but a comparatively short distance away, no tidings whatever could be obtained of the other party who, under Mr. Helmore, had gone to the Makololo tribe.

In June, 1860, Moffat felt that his work at Inyati was done. He had spared neither labour of mind nor body in planting the Mission, and had endured hardships at his advanced age that younger men might well have shrunk from. The hour approached for him to bid a final farewell to Moselekatse, and once more he drew near to the chiefs kraal, with the purpose of speaking to him and his people, for the last time, on the all-important themes of life, death, and eternity. The old chief was in his large courtyard and received his missionary friend kindly. Together they sat, side by side—the Matabele despot, whose name struck terror even then into many native hearts, and the messenger of the Prince of Peace, the warriors ranged themselves in a semi-circle, the women crept as near as they could, and all listened to the last words of "Moshete." It was a solemn service, and closed the long series of efforts which the missionary had made to reach the hearts of Moselekatse and his people. On the morrow he started for home, which he reached in safety, having been absent twelve months.

Meanwhile, terrible trials had befallen the party who had started to found the Makololo Mission. The difficulties attending their journey to Linyanti were such as nothing but the noblest Christian principle would have induced them to encounter, ·

or enabled them to surmount. The chief of these was the great scarcity of water. One of their trials is thus described:—

"From the Zouga we travelled on pretty comfortably, till near the end of November, when we suffered much from want of water.... For more than a week every drop we used had to be walked for about thirty-five miles. Mrs. Helmore's feelings may be imagined, when one afternoon, the thermometer standing at 107 deg. in the shade, she was saving just *one spoonful of water* for each of the dear children for the next morning, not thinking of taking a drop herself. Mr. Helmore, with the men, was then away searching for water; and when he returned the next morning with the precious fluid, we found that he had walked *full forty miles*."

At length, after enduring innumerable difficulties and privations for seven months, they arrived at Linyanti, the residence of the chief Sekeletu. He refused to allow them to remove to a more healthy spot, but proposed that they should live with him in the midst of his fever-generating marshes, and as no better plan offered, they were compelled to accept it. In the course of a week all were laid low with fever. Little Henry Helmore and his sister, with the infant babe of Mr. Price, were the first to die; then followed the heart-stricken mother, Mrs. Helmore; six weeks later Mr. Helmore breathed his last; and the missionary band was reduced to Mr. and Mrs. Price and the helpless orphans. As the only means of saving their lives the survivors prepared to depart, but now the chief threw obstacles in the way of their doing so. Their goods were stolen, their waggon taken possession of; and upon Mr. Price telling the chief that "if they did not let him go soon they would have to bury him beside the others," he was simply told "that he might as well die there as anywhere else."

Finally a few things were allowed for the journey, and the sorrowful party started homeward, Mr. Price very ill, and his wife having lost the use of her feet and legs.

With the scantiest possible provision they had to face a journey of upwards of a thousand miles to Kuruman, but they set forward. Just as they were beginning to take hope after their heavy trials, and to think of renewed efforts for the Lord, Mrs. Price was called to her rest. "My dear wife," wrote the sorrowing husband, "had been for a long time utterly helpless, but we all thought she was getting better. In the morning I found her breathing very hard. She went to sleep that night, alas! to wake no more. I spoke to her, and tried to wake her, but it was too late. I watched her all the morning. She became worse and worse, and a little after mid-day her spirit took its flight to God who gave it. I buried her the same evening under a tree—the only tree on the immense plain of Mahabe. This is indeed a heavy stroke, but 'God is my refuge and strength, a very present help in trouble.'"

Finally the bereaved missionary was met by Mr. and Mrs. Mackenzie, who had started to join the Makololo Mission, and, as all turned their steps towards Kuruman, they were rejoiced by meeting Robert Moffat, who, having heard of the disaster, and that Mr. Price, with the remnant of the party, were on the road, had gone out in search of them. All returned sorrowfully to Kuruman, and the ill-fated Makololo Mission collapsed.

Robert Moffat and his wife watched the progress of the Mission at Inyati with the keenest interest. In it they seemed to live their early life at Lattakoo over again. Their hearts were in the work of the missionaries at that distant station; and, over and above the earnest desire they had to see the work of God prosper among those uncivilised natives, was the tie of kinship, their own flesh and blood being present in the person of their son, John Moffat, who, with his wife, formed a portion of the Matabele Mission. Post-bags and supplies were forwarded by every available opportunity, and warm words of cheer and sympathy from the aged pair at Kuruman encouraged the workers in the far distant region to perseverance in their work for the Lord.

Kuruman served indeed as a home station to which all the interior missionaries could look. The fact of being an interior missionary was sufficient to secure the travel-worn stranger, or friend, a warm welcome and good cheer for weeks together, and none entered more heartily or with deeper sympathy into the plans and endeavours of the wayfarer, or offered more earnest prayers on the behalf of himself and his work, than the tried and faithful couple, Robert and Mary Moffat, who had for so many years borne the burden and heat of the day.

In October, 1861, their daughter Bessie, who was born on board ship in Table Bay, as they were leaving for their first visit to England, married Mr. R. Price, whose wife died the previous year, during that terrible journey from Linyanti, when the Makololo Mission had to be abandoned. Thus as one fell from the ranks, another stepped forward to take the vacant place, and carry on the glorious work for the sake of Him who said, "Go ye into all the world, and preach the Gospel to every creature." The Prices went for a time to Shoshong, hoping to join the Matabele Mission, but finally laboured among the Bakwena, under the chief Sechele.

The Kuruman station itself during this time presented a scene of unabated activity. A revision of the New Testament was in progress, the youngest Miss Moffat, then the only child at home, was working hard at schools and classes, and Mr. Ashton was again at work with his old colleague.

The year 1862 brought severe domestic bereavements to the Moffats. During a journey to Durban, in Natal, their eldest son, Mr. Robert Moffat, died, leaving a wife and four children. He had started to bring them from Durban to the home he had prepared at Kuruman. He had primarily been intended for a missionary, and had been sent to England to be educated for that purpose, but his health failing he had to return to South Africa, where for some time he served in the Survey Department under Government, and afterwards became a trader. He was very highly respected and had thoroughly gained the confidence of the natives.

A few weeks later the sad tidings reached the sorrowing parents from the Zambesi that their eldest daughter Mary, the wife of Dr. Livingstone, had been called to her rest. A white marble cross, near Shupanga House on the Shire River, marks the spot where this sainted martyr to the cause of Africa's regeneration sleeps in peace.

In the following year tidings reached Robert Moffat that William Ross the missionary at Lekatlong, about eighty miles to the south-east, was seriously ill. In a few hours Moffat was on his way; he arrived in time to find his friend alive, and did all that could be done to alleviate his suffering, but shortly after he also passed away. This mournful event led to Mr. Ashton being transferred to Lekatlong, and for a time the whole weight of duty at Kuruman rested on Moffat's shoulders.

Although in perils oft, Robert Moffat had never suffered thus far personal violence from the hands of a native, but now he had a very narrow escape from death. A young man, who for some time had been living on the station, had shown signs of a disordered mind, and was placed under mild restraint. Conceiving a violent personal animosity against the missionary, he attacked him as he was returning from church, and with a knobbed stick inflicted some terrible blows, then, frightened at his own violence, he fled. To one with a weaker frame than Robert Moffat's the consequences might have been very serious; as it was he recovered, though with a heart that was sorely grieved.

In 1865, the Mission was reinforced by the arrival of the Rev. John Brown, from England, and by John Moffat, who had returned from the Matabele. The relaxation from the active duties of the station thus afforded was utilised by Robert Moffat in the work of Scripture revision, the preparation of additional hymns, and the carrying of smaller works through the press.

Mention has been made of the marriage of their second daughter, Ann, to Jean Fredoux, a missionary of the Paris Evangelical Society, who was stationed at Motito, a place situated about thirty-six miles to the north-east of Kuruman. He was a man of gentle disposition and addicted to study. Early in March, 1866, he had started upon a tour to carry on evangelistic work among the Barolong villages along the margin of the Kalahari desert. While visiting one of these, a low class trader arrived who had been guilty of atrocious conduct at Motito. The natives insisted upon the trader going to Kuruman, where his conduct could be investigated, and, upon his refusing to do so, prepared to take him by force. He intrenched himself in his waggon with all his guns loaded, and dared any one to lay hands upon him. Fredoux seeing the serious state that matters were assuming quietly drew near to the trader's waggon, and urged him to go peaceably to Kuruman, assuring him that the people were determined he should go, if not peaceably, then by force.

While thus pleading with this man, a fearful explosion took place, the waggon and its occupant were blown to atoms, Jean Fredoux and twelve natives were killed, and about thirty more were injured.

This was a further heavy affliction for Robert Moffat and his wife. As soon as they heard of the catastrophe, Robert hastened to succour his widowed daughter, and to consign to the grave at Motito the shattered remains of his son-in-law.

A few months later another visit was paid to the open grave, this time to consign to its last resting place the body of Mrs. Brown, the wife of the Rev. John Brown, who a short time before had taken up his abode at the Kuruman as a colleague of Robert Moffat.

In 1868 the missionary staff at that station consisted of Robert Moffat and his son John Moffat. The former had now more than completed the three-score years and ten allotted to man as the duration of human life, and unlike the great leader of

God's chosen people, of whom it is said, "his eye was not dim, nor his natural force abated," Robert Moffat felt the infirmities of age creeping very rapidly upon him. Yet he held on his way for two years longer. A short and constant cough during the winter months aggravated his natural tendency to sleeplessness, and at last he felt himself reluctantly compelled to accept the invitation of the Directors to return finally to England.

Going home to England it could hardly be called, his home was with his loved Bechwanas, with those for whom he had toiled and prayed so long. The ashes of his son Robert, and of his devoted daughter Mary reposed beneath the sands of Africa; his early and later manhood had been spent beneath its scorching sun. The house he was to leave had been the birthplace of most of his children, and his home for more than forty years. Yes, it was hard to leave; and the expectation had become very real to him that his body and that of his faithful partner would be laid side by side in that little burial-ground in the bushy dell, marked by a few trees, at Kuruman. But the final determination had been arrived at, and with slow and hesitating steps, as though waiting for something, even then, to prevent their departure, preparations were made for leaving the station for ever.

Of the general aspect of affairs at the Kuruman during these last two years we have a graphic description from the pen of the Rev. John Moffat, who in a letter to the Directors dated 12th October, 1868, wrote as follows:—

"The public services on the station are a prayer-meeting at sunrise on Sunday; preaching in Sechwana, morning, afternoon, and evening, with the Sunday school twice, and a juvenile afternoon service. The early prayer-meeting is left entirely to the natives, the three preaching services entirely to the missionaries, and the Sunday school, with the juvenile service, to my sister. There is also a Wednesday evening service, a monthly missionary prayer meeting, a church meeting, and a prayer meeting on Thursday afternoon. This last is in the hands of the natives. No native takes any part in the preaching on the station, except in extreme cases, when it is regarded as a makeshift. My father and I share the preaching between us. Occasionally, say once in three weeks, one of us rides to two villages to the north-west, holding services at each; they are respectively eight and twelve miles distant. My custom at home, in the regular way, is to give New Testament reading in the morning, a topical sermon in the afternoon, and Old Testament exposition in the evening. On Monday evening I have a young men's Bible class, which is to me the most interesting work I have to do, more especially as I have much encouragement in it.... On the Monday evening, also, my sister and I hold a practising class for the purpose of trying to improve the singing. On Tuesday evening I meet male inquirers, on Wednesday, before the service, I have a Bible class for women, on Thursday we have an English prayer meeting, and on Friday evening I meet female inquirers. I need not mention the school conducted by my sister and three native assistants."

Speaking of the place and people he continues:—

"The population is small and scattered. On the spot there must be a good many people, and also at the villages to the north-west; but otherwise the district contains only small villages of from twenty to one hundred huts. It extends fifty miles west and north-west, and about twenty-five miles in other directions.

"The people are poor and must remain so. The country is essentially dry. Irrigation is necessary for successful agriculture, and there are few spots where water flows. There is no market for cattle, even if they throve abundantly, which they do not. I despair of much advance in civilisation, when their resources are so small, and when the European trade is on the principle of enormous profits and losses. Two hundred per cent, on Port Elizabeth prices is not considered out of the way.

"Heathenism, as a system, is weak, indeed in many places it is nowhere. Christianity meets with little opposition. The people generally are prodigious Bible readers, church-goers, and psalm-singers, I fear to a large extent without knowledge. Religion to them consists in the above operations, and in giving a sum to the Auxiliary. I am speaking of the generality, There are many whom I cannot but feel to be Christians, but dimly. This can hardly be the result of low mental power alone. The Bechwanas show considerable acuteness when circumstances call it out.

"The educational department of the Mission has been kept in the background. On this station the youth on leaving school have sunk back for want of a continued course being opened to them. The village schoolmasters, uneducated themselves, and mostly unpaid, make but a feeble impression. The wonder is that they do so much, and where the readers come from. It is hard to say that the older missionaries could have done otherwise.... I cannot tell you how one thing presses on me every day: the want of qualified native schoolmasters and teachers; and the question: how are they to be obtained?"

MAIN STREET IN PORT ELIZABETH.

On Sunday, 20th March, 1870, Robert Moffat preached for the last time in the Kuruman church, and on the Friday following the departure took place. "Ramary" and "Mamary," as Mr. and Mrs. Moffat were called, had completely won the hearts of the natives. For weeks past messages of farewell had been coming from the more distant towns and villages, and now that the final hour had arrived and the venerable missionary, with his long white beard, and his equally revered wife, left their house and walked to their waggon they were beset by crowds of people, each one longing for another shake of the hand, a last parting word, or a final look; and, as the waggon drove away, a long pitiful wail rose from those who felt that their teacher and friend was with them no more.

After a rough but safe journey of eight weeks, Robert and Mary Moffat reached Port Elizabeth on the 20th May, 1870, and received a hearty welcome from a large number of missionaries and other Christian friends, who had gathered to meet them. Making a brief stay they embarked in the mail steamer ***Roman*** and landed at Cape Town on the 2nd of June. Here they were entertained by the Christian community at a public breakfast. A few days later they embarked in the steamship ***Norseman***, ***en route*** for England.

CHAPTER X
CLOSING SCENES

In the Chronicle of the London Missionary Society for March, 1870, the following notice appeared: "Our readers will be glad to hear that there is now a definite prospect of welcoming again to England our veteran missionary, the Rev. Robert Moffat. He may be expected, with Mrs. Moffat, about the month of June. Mr. Moffat no longer enjoys his former robust health. In his last letter he writes: 'What to me was formerly a molehill is now a mountain, and we both have for some time past begun to feel some of the labour and sorrow so frequently experienced by those who have passed their three-score years and ten.'"

The *Norseman* reached Plymouth on the 24th of July, and next day Robert and Mary Moffat landed at Southampton, thus returning to their native land, to leave it no more, after an absence of over fifty years; during which time they had visited it only once before.

On the 1st of August he was welcomed by the Society, at an influential meeting, convened for the purpose, in the Board Room of the Mission House, in Blomfield Street. At that meeting, alluding to his previous visit in 1839, and to the printing of the New Testament in Sechwana, he stated as follows:—

"When I came to the Cape, previous to my first visit, I brought a translation of the New Testament, which I had translated under considerable difficulties, being engaged a portion of the day in roofing an immense church, and the remainder in exegetical examinations and consulting concordances. I was anxious to get it printed, and I brought it down to the Cape, but there I could find no printing-office that would undertake it. The Committee of the Bible Society very kindly—as they have always been to me, I say it with pleasure—forwarded paper and ink to the Cape expecting I should get the work done there. As I said, there was not a printing-office that would undertake it. Dining with Sir George Napier, the Governor, I informed him of the difficulty. He said, 'Jump on board a ship with your translation and get it printed in England, and you will be back again while they are thinking about it here. Print a New Testament among a set of Dutch printers! why I can't even get my proclamations printed.' I said, 'I have become too barbarous; I have almost forgotten my own language; I should be frightened to go there.' 'Oh stuff!' he said.

"Some time after he met me in the street: 'Well, Moffat, what have you determined upon?' 'I am waiting the return of Dr. Philip.' 'Don't wait for anybody; just jump on board a ship. Think of the importance of getting the New Testament put in print in a new language!' He invited me to dinner again and said, 'Have you come to a conclusion? I wish I could give you mine. I feel some interest in the extension of the knowledge of the Word of God. Take nobody's advice, but jump on board a ship for England.' He spoke so seriously that I began to feel serious myself.

"Dr. Philip came, and when the Governor explained the circumstances, the Doctor said, 'Go, by all means.' I was nervous at the thought. I was not a nervous man in Africa. I could sleep and hear the lions roar. There seemed so many great folks to meet with. I came to England and by-and-by I got over it."

On the Wednesday, following this meeting, he was entertained at a public breakfast at the Cannon Street Hotel.

For a few weeks the Moffats dwelt at Canonbury, though Robert himself was so much engaged in visiting different parts of the country, Edinburgh included, where he met with many old friends, that he was not suffered at this time to dwell for long in any one place.

The winter was spent at Brixton, and on the 21st of December, L1000 was presented to Robert Moffat as a birthday gift, a most cheering tribute of esteem to a tried and faithful servant of Jesus Christ.

The effects of this act of kindness had not passed away when a heavy cloud hung over the happy home at Brixton. She, who for more than half-a-century had been the loving helpmeet of the African missionary, sharing his joys and sorrows, his hopes and discouragements, and many of his privations and perils, lay dying. A troublesome cough, a difficulty of breathing, a few long deep breaths, and she was gone, without even a word of farewell; called home to receive the "Well done, good and faithful servant," and to enter into the joy of her Lord.

MARY MOFFAT.

Her last words were a prayer for her husband, that strength might be given him to bear the blow.

Robert Moffat indeed needed strength in this hour of affliction. His first exclamation on finding that she had really gone was, "For fifty-three years I have had her to pray for me," and writing to his old friend and fellow-labourer, Roger Edwards, who was then at Port Elizabeth, he said, "How lonely I feel, and if it were not for Jeanie (his daughter) it would be much more so."

The events of the next few years may be briefly summarised. He travelled much to different parts of the country, visiting High Leigh, the old house at Dukinfield, and Carronshore. His services were continually in requisition for missionary meetings, and doubtless many of our readers will be old enough to remember the bronzed face, with its full flowing beard, blanched by age, the keen eyes, and the venerable form of Robert Moffat at this time, and to call to mind the pleasure they derived as they listened to his glowing descriptions of the needs of Africa.

The winter of 1871 was passed at Ventnor, in the Isle of Wight, and occupied in revising proof sheets of the Old Testament in Sechwana. While there he was, by Her Majesty's own desire, introduced to the Queen, whom he had never seen before. He also received the degree of Doctor of Divinity, from the University of Edinburgh.

To meet the need for training a native ministry, which had been felt by Moffat and others engaged in the work of the Bechwana Mission, and which had shortly before his return been pressed upon the attention of the Directors, several thousand pounds were subscribed, and, as a way of doing honour to the veteran who was now in their midst, it was proposed to call the Institute that was to be founded, "The Moffat Institute." This now stands as a centre of influence amidst the tribes surrounding the Kuruman station.

In 1873, a number of friends, who thought that the liberal contributions which had been subscribed to the Institute, hardly gave such a direct proof of their esteem for their venerated friend as could be desired, presented Robert Moffat with a sum of upwards of L5000. This liberality provided for his wants during the remainder of his life, enabled him to serve the Directors and the cause of missions, without being any longer a burden upon the funds of the Society, and also placed him in a position to meet the wants of his widowed daughter and her fatherless family.

While living at Brixton, Robert Moffat attended the ministry of the late Rev. Baldwin Brown, in whose mission-work in Lambeth he was much interested. On his eightieth birthday, 21st December, 1875, he opened the new Mission Hall in connection with this work, which hall was thenceforward called by his name. On the same day he received many congratulatory tokens, among them being an address signed by a great number of Congregational ministers from every part of the country. Prior to this in the same year, he had lectured upon Missions in Westminster Abbey, and in the preceding year he had performed the melancholy duty of identifying the remains of his son-in-law, Dr. Livingstone, upon their being brought home from Africa.

Engagements and constant requests for his services made great inroads upon his time. "People either could not or would not see that he was getting old," he frequently said; but people knew that as long as he had strength to speak, he would not grow weary of addressing audiences on missionary work.

In 1876, we find him dining on one occasion with the Archbishop of Canterbury at Lambeth Palace, and on another breakfasting with Mr. Gladstone, in the house of the Rev. Newman Hall. In the following year by invitation of the French Missionary Society he visited Paris, and while there addressed a meeting of 4000 Sunday-school children.

On the 20th of December, 1878, he received the freedom of the City of London, and somewhat over two years later was the guest of the then Lord Mayor, Alderman, now Sir William, McArthur, for several days, a banquet being given in his honour.

During the time that Cetewayo was in England Robert Moffat was much interested in him and paid him a visit. Among the Zulu king's attendants was a man who could speak Sechwana, and with him Moffat at once got into conversation. The man's delight was unbounded. He had been in the train of a son of Moselekatse, and had heard of the missionary. "A u Moshete?" (Are you Moffat) he asked again and again, with beaming eyes exclaiming when convinced of the fact, "I see this day what my eyes never expected to behold, Moshete!"

For the last four years of his life Robert Moffat resided at Park Cottage, Leigh, near Tunbridge, where he was the tenant of the late Samuel Morley, Esq. From both Mr. and Mrs. Morley he received much kindness, which continued until the day of his death.

The end now drew near. In 1883, he complained of great weariness and intermittent pulsation. This troubled him so constantly that advice was sought. For a short time this availed. He attended the Bible Society's meeting in the second week in May, and the meeting of the London Missionary Society on the 10th, and in July paid a visit to Knockholt, where he met Mr. and Mrs. George Sturge. From this visit he returned seeming better, but in a few days unfavourable symptoms again showed themselves. Yet the strong frame, that had endured so much, seemed loath to give in, and, whenever able, he was in and out of his garden. He also took two drives, Mrs. Morley very kindly sending her carriage for that purpose when he felt able to make use of it.

"Mark the perfect man, and behold the upright: for the end of that man is peace." Most beautifully was this truth exemplified in the closing scenes of the life of this truly noble and good man. On Sunday, 5th August, he was too weak to attend chapel, and spent a peaceful Sabbath at home. He was very fond of hymns and would often repeat one after another. In the evening he chose several which were sung, though feebleness prevented him from joining the singing. Among those chosen were: "The sands of time are sinking," "Come, Thou fount of every blessing," "How sweet the name of Jesus sounds," and "Nearer, my God, to Thee." His New Testament was his constant companion during these last days, and whatever the topic of conversation, it always turned with him to heaven and the Saviour.

On Monday he seemed somewhat better, but on Tuesday night he was much worse. Hours of pain and sleeplessness were passed, yet he rose on Wednesday and went out several times to the garden. In the evening he became very ill and had a fainting fit, but managed after awhile to get upstairs, and, after remaining on the bedside for some time, propped up with pillows, he undressed, with little assistance and much deliberation, winding up his watch, with a cold, trembling hand,—"for the last time," he said.

The doctor arrived shortly afterwards, who found that he had broken a blood-vessel. The night was passed partly in peaceful sleep, and partly in converse with his children who were then present. His daughter says, "He was just full of his Saviour's love and mercy all through his life; he repeated many hymns and passages of Scripture."

On Thursday morning he was visited by Mr. Morley and two other friends, with whom he conversed. He also had his Testament, but finding he could not read it, his daughters read to him. He repeated many hymns, among them the Scotch version of the hundred and third Psalm, but stopped and said, "There is nothing like the original," which was then read from the Bible. His mother's favourite hymn, "Hail, sovereign Light," was also by his special desire read to him.

Another sleep—a wandering, perhaps unconscious, look at his children, a struggle, and then a quietness? and the pilgrimage was over, the spirit had fled to be present with the Lord whom he had loved so well and served so faithfully. "His end was peace."

He died on the 10th of August, 1883, in his eighty-eighth year.

The funeral took place a few days later at Norwood Cemetery, when, surrounded by such relatives as were in England, Sir Bartle Frere, Mr. Samuel Morley and several other Members of Parliament, deputations from the various Missionary and several Religious Societies, and by the Mayor of Bloemfontein, his remains were consigned to the tomb.

Never had a truer hero been borne to the grave, nor one more thoroughly worthy of the name of MAN.

CHAPTER XI
CONCLUSION

As soon as it was realised that Robert Moffat had actually gone, it was felt that a truly great man had departed from among us. A niche in the temple of earth's true nobility seemed empty. The prevailing feeling was given expression to by some of the leading journals, which in eulogistic articles commented upon the life, work, and character of him who had gone.

The Times, in its review, contained the following remarks:—"His chief work was among the Bechwanas. His picture of what they were when he first knew them would hardly now be recognised, so entirely have they changed under the new influences which Moffat was the first to bring to bear upon them. He found them mere savages, constantly at war among themselves and with their neighbours, ignorant of the arts of agriculture, and in the utterly degraded state for which we must seek a counterpart now in the more distant tribes, whom the message of civilisation has not yet reached. His first care was to make himself thoroughly master of the language of those to whom he was sent. For fifty years he has declared he had been accustomed to speak the Bechwana tongue; he reduced it to written characters, and translated the Scriptures into it. The Bechwanas, under Moffat's guidance, became new men. Mission work grew and spread among them; what Moffat had begun to do was taken up by other hands; a permanent body of native pastors was created from among the Bechwanas themselves, and the whole region was raised out of the savage state in which Moffat had found it, and became, in no small degree, civilised as well as Christianised.... It would seem, indeed, that it is only by the agency of such men as Moffat and his like that the contact of the white and black races can be anything but a curse to the blacks. It is the missionary alone who seeks nothing for himself. He has chosen an unselfish life. If honour comes to him, it is by no choice of his own, but as the unsought tribute which others, as it were, force upon him. Robert Moffat has died in the fullness both of years and honours. His work has been to lay the foundations of the Church in the central regions of South Africa. As far as his influence and that of his coadjutors and successors has extended, it has brought with it unmixed good. His name will be remembered while the South African Church endures, and his example will remain with us as a stimulus to others, and as an abiding proof of what a Christian missionary can be and can do."

The **Brighton Daily News** commenced its article by saying:—"The grave has just closed over one of the most notable men whose figures are familiar to the inhabitants of Brighton. Robert Moffat, the veteran pioneer in the mission field, and the simplest of heroes, has passed away, and many of the noblest of the land followed his remains to their resting-place." It concluded with, "In the drawing-rooms of fashionable Brighton, crowded with the lovers of art and science, no one grudged the cessation of music the most classical, or of conversation the most charming, to listen to the venerable Doctor when requested to repeat some incidents of his missionary life. All felt that the scene was hallowed by the presence of one who had done a work for the good of men, such as few have been privileged to accomplish. Robert Moffat belonged to no sect or party. To better the world and advance the one Church formed the sole end of his being."

Other journals and magazines bore like testimony to his worth.

Of his work we have said much in the preceding pages, and also something of its results. To this may be added Robert Moffat's own account of some of the benefits which sprung from the prosecution of missionary enterprise in South Africa. In his speech at Port Elizabeth, on finally leaving for England, in May, 1870, referring to the general progress made in the interior, he said:—

"Christianity has already accomplished much in this long benighted land. When I first went to the Kuruman scarcely an individual could go beyond. Now they travel in safety to the Zambesi. Then we were strangers, and they could not comprehend us. They treated us with great indignity, and considered us to be the outcasts of society, who, being driven from our own race, went to reside with them; but bearing in remembrance what our Saviour had to undergo, we were encouraged to persevere, and much success has rewarded our efforts. Now it is safe to traverse any part of the country, and traders travel far beyond Kuruman without the slightest fear of molestation. Formerly men of one tribe could not travel through another's territory, and wars were frequent. During my early mission life, I often heard of men of one tribe going to trade with another, and being murdered. I was at a native place when a thing of that sort once occurred. A party of men had come two hundred miles to dispose of some articles. The resident natives, taking a dislike to them, set upon them and killed two of their number. I asked them why they had done this, and tried to show them it was wrong. They seemed to know that; and from that time I have never heard of anything of the sort.

"The influence of Christianity in that country is now very great, and constantly increasing. Where one station was scarcely tolerated, there are now several. The Moravians have their missionaries. The Berlin Society have theirs, and others are engaged in the good work, besides numerous native Gospel teachers. Our advanced station at the Matabele is in a very prosperous state, and I quite expect that the Matabele will become one day a great nation. They sternly obey their own laws, and I have noticed that when men of fixed principles become convinced of the great truths of Christianity they hold firmly to the faith, and their fidelity is not lightly to be shaken."

In the same speech he also mentioned the fact that whereas at first the natives would not buy anything, not even a pocket handkerchief, now, when he was speaking, no less than sixty thousand pounds worth of British manufactures passed yearly into the hands of the native tribes around Kuruman.

Thus the missionary prepared the way for the merchant, and the Gospel for the progress of civilisation.

Of Moffat's character we have had frequent glimpses in the preceding pages; of his personal appearance and dignified mien our portrait and pictures give some idea. A few words may, however, be added, based upon the facts recorded by his son in the last chapter of "Robert and Mary Moffat."

Tall and strong, with dark piercing eyes, he stood, a man of dauntless courage, quick and energetic in action, with a resolution in the performance of duty that no opposition could thwart; yet, withal, of gentle manner, and of an even temper, proof against the many attacks made upon it. His disposition was to think well of men, and to believe what they said. Deceit he hated, it was the one thing he could not forgive. He trusted men implicitly; and this probably accounted for the fact that the Bechwanas, who carried the art of lying to perfection, seldom lied to him. They knew it was the one thing that would make him angry.

His reverence for holy things was very great. He relished a joke as well as any man, indeed, there was a good deal of humour in him; but woe to that man who spoke jestingly of the things pertaining to God. The Word of the Lord was too real and too important for any triviality. God was ever present to him, and he lived for God. His son says: "Even when I was alone with him, on some of his itinerating journeys, no meal was commenced without a reverent doffing of the Scotch bonnet, his usual head-dress in those days, and the solemn blessing; and our morning and evening worship was never missed or hurried."

An instance of his forbearance under provocation is afforded in the following:—

"On our return from England in 1843," says the writer just quoted, "we were a large party, with three or four waggons. One night we outspanned in the dark, not knowing that we were on forbidden ground—within the limits of a farm, but a half-mile short of the homestead. In the early morning a young man rode up, and demanded to know what we were doing there without leave. My father gently explained that we had done it in ignorance, but his explanation was cut short by a harangue loud and long. The stripling sat on his horse, my father stood before him with bowed head and folded arms, whilst a torrent of abuse poured over him, with a plentiful mixture of such terse and biting missiles of invective as greatly enrich the South African Dutch language. We stood around and remembered that only a few months before the man thus rated like a dog was standing before enthusiastic thousands in England, who hung with bated breath upon his utterances. Something of shame must have arrested the wrath of the young man, for he suddenly rode away without impounding our cattle, as he had threatened to do. We inspanned and proceeded, calling on our way at the house, and there we found ourselves received by a venerable white-haired farmer and his wife with open arms, for they and my parents proved to be old friends. Right glad were we that nothing had been done on our side to make us ashamed to meet them."

In his home he was a true father, and the influence that surrounded his children must have been a happy one, seeing that so many of them embraced the missionary calling, and followed in the footsteps of their venerated parents. Mary, the eldest daughter, married Dr. Livingstone; Ann, the French missionary, Jean Fredoux; Bessie, a younger daughter, was united to the Rev. Roger Price; and a son, the Rev. John Moffat, became for a time his father's coadjutor at the Kuruman station.

In bringing this memoir to a conclusion, we may be permitted to glance at South Africa as it is at the present time, and to note some of the contrasts between its condition now, and that as stated in our opening chapter, prior to Robert Moffat's arrival. At the time when he first landed at Cape Town, the work of evangelising the heathen was confined principally to two Societies—the Moravian Mission and the London Missionary Society. Now the Societies exceed twelve in number, and represent the following nationalities: English, American, French, Swiss, Norwegian, and the people of Finland.

First, in order of date, may be noticed the work of the Moravian Brethren, which is chiefly carried on among the Hottentots and Kafirs. Their chief station is Genadendal, eighty miles east of Cape Town, which has several smaller stations grouped around it. Besides these, still farther east, among the Kafir tribes, is the station of Shiloh, also having a number of out-stations gathered round it.

The London Missionary Society follows with its eleven principal stations and nine out-stations. This Society is now labouring in South Africa, in Kafirland, Bechwanaland and Matabeleland. The Report for 1886 shows sixteen English missionaries and sixty-five native preachers as engaged in preaching and teaching, and as results, 1361 Church members. These returns are however incomplete, and very much has occurred, through the numerous wars and unsettled state of the country, to retard the progress of missionary work.

Next comes the Wesleyan Missionary Society, who, commencing operations at Cape Town in 1814, extended their stations round the coast from Little Namaqualand to Zululand. They are also labouring among the Barolongs in the Orange Free State, in Swaziland, and at the Gold Fields at Barberton, in the Transvaal.

The Scotch Presbyterians are represented by the missions of the Free Church of Scotland, and the United Presbyterian Church. These confine their labours principally to British Kaffraria and Kafirland. The Free Church has a high-class Institution at Lovedale for the training of a native ministry and also for teaching the natives many of the useful arts, and an improved system of agriculture. There is an efficient staff of teachers, and in 1885, 380 pupils attended the Institution, of whom seventy-one were Church members and ninety-one candidates or inquirers. A similar institution has also been established among the Fingoes at Blythswood in Fingoland.

More than fifty years ago, at the suggestion of Dr. Philip, the Rhenish Mission commenced work among the Hottentots of Cape Colony, but its operations extended, and now embrace Little and Great Namaqualand, south and north of the Orange River, and, away beyond, the territory known as Damaraland. Their stations are in a flourishing condition, and some 15,000 converts bear evidence to the success of their efforts. This Society also looks after the preparation of native teachers, &c., and has an excellent institution for that purpose at Worcester, near Cape Town, its principal station.

Still farther north, beyond Damaraland is Ovampoland, occupied by the Missionary Society of Finland. Seven ordained Missionaries and three Christian artisans were equipped and despatched to work in this region, at the suggestion of the Rhenish Society. Their enterprise is of comparatively recent date and results cannot yet be tabulated. The influence for good exerted will, however, doubtless yield fruit by-and-by.

The missions of the Berlin Society stretch from the eastern portion of Cape Colony to the Transvaal, and embrace also the Orange Free State and the Diamond Fields. They have over 7000 converts, and a large number of children under instruction in various schools.

Basutoland, to the east of the Orange Free State, is cared for by the French Evangelical Missionary Society, who commenced work in South Africa in 1829. Their first missionaries were appointed to the Bahurutse, then tributary to Moselekatse, but being repulsed through the jealousy of that potentate they settled at Motito, and finally accepted an invitation from Moshesh, chief of the Basutos, to work among that people. The mission has fourteen principal stations and sixty-six out-stations, with about 20,000 adherents, of whom about 3500 are Church members.

In 1835 six missionaries, appointed by the American Board of Foreign Missions, arrived from the United States to labour in South Africa. Three proceeded to Natal and settled near Durban. The other three journeyed to Moselekatse at Mosega. Their mission was however broken up through the incursions of the Boers, and they were compelled to flee to Natal. For some years the mission there was much harassed through war, but it is now firmly established and is doing excellent work of a religious and educational character, having a number of well-instructed native pastors and teachers, besides the staff of European missionaries. In 1886 the Board reports having in connection with this mission seven stations and seventeen out-stations, and 886 Church members.

The Society for the Propagation of the Gospel commenced its missions in South Africa in 1838. Its work is divided between the Colonists and the natives, and is car-ried on in Cape Colony and Natal; its dioceses stretching round the coast much in the same manner as the Wesleyan stations.

Besides those already mentioned, there are at work now in South Africa the Norwegian Missionary Society, labouring in Natal and Zululand; the Hermannsburg Mission, founded by Pastor Harms, whose operations are carried on in Natal, Zululand, and the Transvaal; and the Swiss society, The Mission of the Free Church of the Canton de Vaud, whose efforts are directed to a tribe inhabiting a country between Delagoa Bay and Sofala.[2]

Thus the missionary cause has grown, notwithstanding the many difficulties it has had to contend with, and now the sound of the Gospel is heard throughout the land. From the southernmost part of what was the "Dark Continent," but which is now termed by some the "Twilight Continent," and which we trust may soon be blessed with the full light of Christianity, there stretches away a series of mission stations right to the Zambesi; and there joining hands with the system of Central African missions the glad tidings of salvation are wafted onward to the great lake, the Victoria Nyanza, in the north; eastward to the coast; and, in the west, made known to thousands by means of the various organisations now doing such excel-lent work on the Congo River.

In a central position, amidst the tribes of South Africa, Kuruman, the scene of Robert Moffat's trials and triumphs, stands to-day, surrounded by a number of na-tive towns and villages, where native teachers, trained in the Moffat Institute, are located, and native Churches have been formed,—a beacon shedding its glorious rays around, dispelling the darkness, and bringing the heathen to the knowledge of the Saviour, Jesus Christ.

THE END

---

2   Many of the facts contained in this review of Mission work in South Africa have been gleaned from "South Africa," by the Rev. James Sibree, F.R.G.S.

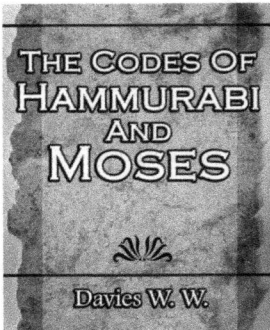

The Codes Of Hammurabi And Moses
W. W. Davies

QTY

The discovery of the Hammurabi Code is one of the greatest achievements of archaeology, and is of paramount interest, not only to the student of the Bible, but also to all those interested in ancient history...

Religion   ISBN: *1-59462-338-4*   **Pages:132**
MSRP $12.95

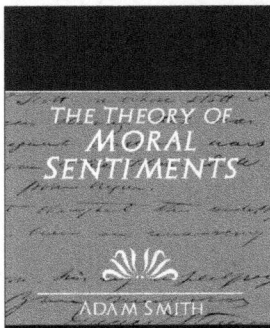

The Theory of Moral Sentiments
Adam Smith

QTY

This work from 1749. contains original theories of conscience amd moral judgment and it is the foundation for systemof morals.

Philosophy ISBN: *1-59462-777-0*   **Pages:536**
MSRP $19.95

Jessica's First Prayer
Hesba Stretton

QTY

In a screened and secluded corner of one of the many railway-bridges which span the streets of London there could be seen a few years ago, from five o'clock every morning until half past eight, a tidily set-out coffee-stall, consisting of a trestle and board, upon which stood two large tin cans, with a small fire of charcoal burning under each so as to keep the coffee boiling during the early hours of the morning when the work-people were thronging into the city on their way to their daily toil...

Childrens   ISBN: *1-59462-373-2*   **Pages:84**
MSRP $9.95

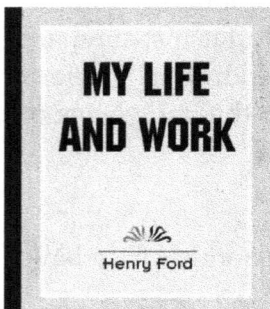

My Life and Work
Henry Ford

QTY

Henry Ford revolutionized the world with his implementation of mass production for the Model T automobile. Gain valuable business insight into his life and work with his own auto-biography... "We have only started on our development of our country we have not as yet, with all our talk of wonderful progress, done more than scratch the surface. The progress has been wonderful enough but..."

Biographies/   ISBN: *1-59462-198-5*   **Pages:300**
MSRP $21.95

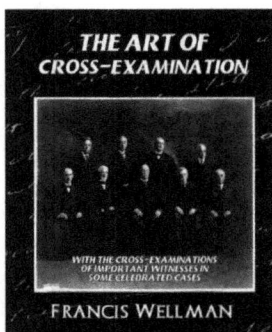

The Art of Cross-Examination
Francis Wellman

QTY

I presume it is the experience of every author, after his first book is published upon an important subject, to be almost overwhelmed with a wealth of ideas and illustrations which could readily have been included in his book, and which to his own mind, at least, seem to make a second edition inevitable. Such certainly was the case with me; and when the first edition had reached its sixth impression in five months, I rejoiced to learn that it seemed to my publishers that the book had met with a sufficiently favorable reception to justify a second and considerably enlarged edition. ..

Reference   ISBN: *1-59462-647-2*

Pages:412
MSRP $19.95

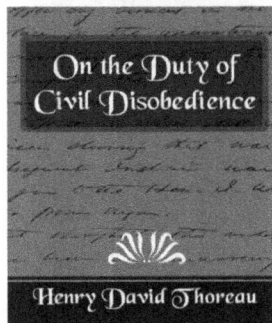

On the Duty of Civil Disobedience
Henry David Thoreau

QTY

Thoreau wrote his famous essay, On the Duty of Civil Disobedience, as a protest against an unjust but popular war and the immoral but popular institution of slave-owning. He did more than write—he declined to pay his taxes, and was hauled off to gaol in consequence. Who can say how much this refusal of his hastened the end of the war and of slavery ?

Law   ISBN: *1-59462-747-9*

Pages:48
MSRP $7.45

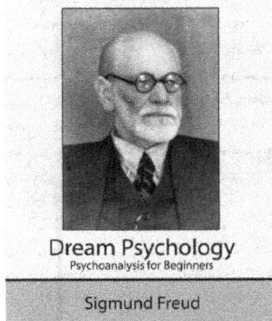

Dream Psychology Psychoanalysis for Beginners
Sigmund Freud

QTY

Sigmund Freud, born Sigismund Schlomo Freud (May 6, 1856 - September 23, 1939), was a Jewish-Austrian neurologist and psychiatrist who co-founded the psychoanalytic school of psychology. Freud is best known for his theories of the unconscious mind, especially involving the mechanism of repression; his redefinition of sexual desire as mobile and directed towards a wide variety of objects; and his therapeutic techniques, especially his understanding of transference in the therapeutic relationship and the presumed value of dreams as sources of insight into unconscious desires.

Psychology   ISBN: *1-59462-905-6*

Pages:196
MSRP $15.45

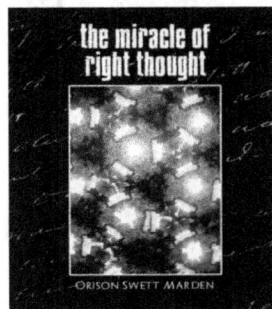

The Miracle of Right Thought
Orison Swett Marden

QTY

Believe with all of your heart that you will do what you were made to do. When the mind has once formed the habit of holding cheerful, happy, prosperous pictures, it will not be easy to form the opposite habit. It does not matter how improbable or how far away this realization may see, or how dark the prospects may be, if we visualize them as best we can, as vividly as possible, hold tenaciously to them and vigorously struggle to attain them, they will gradually become actualized, realized in the life. But a desire, a longing without endeavor, a yearning abandoned or held indifferently will vanish without realization.

Self Help   ISBN: *1-59462-644-8*

Pages:360
MSRP $25.45

QTY

☐ **The Rosicrucian Cosmo-Conception Mystic Christianity** *by Max Heindel*   ISBN: *1-59462-188-8*   **$38.95**
The Rosicrucian Cosmo-conception is not dogmatic, neither does it appeal to any other authority than the reason of the student. It is: not controversial, but is: sent forth in the, hope that it may help to clear...   New Age/Religion Pages 646

☐ **Abandonment To Divine Providence** *by Jean-Pierre de Caussade*   ISBN: *1-59462-228-0*   **$25.95**
"The Rev. Jean Pierre de Caussade was one of the most remarkable spiritual writers of the Society of Jesus in France in the 18th Century. His death took place at Toulouse in 1751. His works have gone through many editions and have been republished...   Inspirational/Religion Pages 400

☐ **Mental Chemistry** *by Charles Haanel*   ISBN: *1-59462-192-6*   **$23.95**
Mental Chemistry allows the change of material conditions by combining and appropriately utilizing the power of the mind. Much like applied chemistry creates something new and unique out of careful combinations of chemicals the mastery of mental chemistry...   New Age Pages 354

☐ **The Letters of Robert Browning and Elizabeth Barret Barrett 1845-1846 vol II**   ISBN: *1-59462-193-4*   **$35.95**
by Robert Browning and Elizabeth Barrett   Biographies Pages 596

☐ **Gleanings In Genesis (volume I)** *by Arthur W. Pink*   ISBN: *1-59462-130-6*   **$27.45**
Appropriately has Genesis been termed "the seed plot of the Bible" for in it we have, in germ form, almost all of the great doctrines which are afterwards fully developed in the books of Scripture which follow...   Religion/Inspirational Pages 420

☐ **The Master Key** *by L. W. de Laurence*   ISBN: *1-59462-001-6*   **$30.95**
In no branch of human knowledge has there been a more lively increase of the spirit of research during the past few years than in the study of Psychology, Concentration and Mental Discipline. The requests for authentic lessons in Thought Control, Mental Discipline and...   New Age/Business Pages 422

☐ **The Lesser Key Of Solomon Goetia** *by L. W. de Laurence*   ISBN: *1-59462-092-X*   **$9.95**
This translation of the first book of the "Lernegton" which is now for the first time made accessible to students of Talismanic Magic was done, after careful collation and edition, from numerous Ancient Manuscripts in Hebrew, Latin, and French...   New Age/Occult Pages 92

☐ **Rubaiyat Of Omar Khayyam** *by Edward Fitzgerald*   ISBN:*1-59462-332-5*   **$13.95**
Edward Fitzgerald, whom the world has already learned, in spite of his own efforts to remain within the shadow of anonymity, to look upon as one of the rarest poets of the century, was born at Bredfield, in Suffolk, on the 31st of March, 1809. He was the third son of John Purcell...   Music Pages 172

☐ **Ancient Law** *by Henry Maine*   ISBN: *1-59462-128-4*   **$29.95**
The chief object of the following pages is to indicate some of the earliest ideas of mankind, as they are reflected in Ancient Law, and to point out the relation of those ideas to modern thought.   Religion/History Pages 452

☐ **Far-Away Stories** *by William J. Locke*   ISBN: *1-59462-129-2*   **$19.45**
"Good wine needs no bush, but a collection of mixed vintages does. And this book is just such a collection. Some of the stories I do not want to remain buried for ever in the museum files of dead magazine-numbers an author's not unpardonable vanity..."   Fiction Pages 272

☐ **Life of David Crockett** *by David Crockett*   ISBN: *1-59462-250-7*   **$27.45**
"Colonel David Crockett was one of the most remarkable men of the times in which he lived. Born in humble life, but gifted with a strong will, an indomitable courage, and unremitting perseverance...   Biographies/New Age Pages 424

☐ **Lip-Reading** *by Edward Nitchie*   ISBN: *1-59462-206-X*   **$25.95**
Edward B. Nitchie, founder of the New York School for the Hard of Hearing, now the Nitchie School of Lip-Reading, Inc, wrote "LIP-READING Principles and Practice". The development and perfecting of this meritorious work on lip-reading was an undertaking...   How-to Pages 400

☐ **A Handbook of Suggestive Therapeutics, Applied Hypnotism, Psychic Science**   ISBN: *1-59462-214-0*   **$24.95**
by Henry Munro   Health/New Age/Health/Self-help Pages 376

☐ **A Doll's House: and Two Other Plays** *by Henrik Ibsen*   ISBN: *1-59462-112-8*   **$19.95**
Henrik Ibsen created this classic when in revolutionary 1848 Rome. Introducing some striking concepts in playwriting for the realist genre, this play has been studied the world over.   Fiction/Classics/Plays 308

☐ **The Light of Asia** *by sir Edwin Arnold*   ISBN: *1-59462-204-3*   **$13.95**
In this poetic masterpiece, Edwin Arnold describes the life and teachings of Buddha. The man who was to become known as Buddha to the world was born as Prince Gautama of India but he rejected the worldly riches and abandoned the reigns of power when...   Religion/History/Biographies Pages 170

☐ **The Complete Works of Guy de Maupassant** *by Guy de Maupassant*   ISBN: *1-59462-157-8*   **$16.95**
"For days and days, nights and nights, I had dreamed of that first kiss which was to consecrate our engagement, and I knew not on what spot I should put my lips..."   Fiction/Classics Pages 240

☐ **The Art of Cross-Examination** *by Francis L. Wellman*   ISBN: *1-59462-309-0*   **$26.95**
Written by a renowned trial lawyer, Wellman imparts his experience and uses case studies to explain how to use psychology to extract desired information through questioning.   How-to/Science/Reference Pages 408

☐ **Answered or Unanswered?** *by Louisa Vaughan*   ISBN: *1-59462-248-5*   **$10.95**
Miracles of Faith in China   Religion Pages 112

☐ **The Edinburgh Lectures on Mental Science (1909)** *by Thomas*   ISBN: *1-59462-008-3*   **$11.95**
This book contains the substance of a course of lectures recently given by the writer in the Queen Street Hall, Edinburgh. Its purpose is to indicate the Natural Principles governing the relation between Mental Action and Material Conditions...   New Age/Psychology Pages 148

☐ **Ayesha** *by H. Rider Haggard*   ISBN: *1-59462-301-5*   **$24.95**
Verily and indeed it is the unexpected that happens! Probably if there was one person upon the earth from whom the Editor of this, and of a certain previous history, did not expect to hear again...   Classics Pages 380

☐ **Ayala's Angel** *by Anthony Trollope*   ISBN: *1-59462-352-X*   **$29.95**
The two girls were both pretty, but Lucy who was twenty-one who supposed to be simple and comparatively unattractive, whereas Ayala was credited, as her Bombwhat romantic name might show, with poetic charm and a taste for romance. Ayala when her father died was nineteen...   Fiction Pages 484

☐ **The American Commonwealth** *by James Bryce*   ISBN: *1-59462-286-8*   **$34.45**
An interpretation of American democratic political theory. It examines political mechanics and society from the perspective of Scotsman James Bryce   Politics Pages 572

☐ **Stories of the Pilgrims** *by Margaret P. Pumphrey*   ISBN: *1-59462-116-0*   **$17.95**
This book explores pilgrims religious oppression in England as well as their escape to Holland and eventual crossing to America on the Mayflower, and their early days in New England...   History Pages 268

QTY

The Fasting Cure *by Sinclair Upton*   ISBN: *1-59462-222-1* **$13.95**
In the Cosmopolitan Magazine for May, 1910, and in the Contemporary Review (London) for April, 1910, I published an article dealing with my experiences in fasting. I have written a great many magazine articles, but never one which attracted so much attention... New Age/Self Help/Health Pages 164

Hebrew Astrology *by Sepharial*   ISBN: *1-59462-308-2* **$13.45**
In these days of advanced thinking it is a matter of common observation that we have left many of the old landmarks behind and that we are now pressing forward to greater heights and to a wider horizon than that which represented the mind-content of our progenitors... Astrology Pages 144

Thought Vibration or The Law of Attraction in the Thought World   ISBN: *1-59462-127-6* **$12.95**
by William Walker Atkinson   Psychology/Religion Pages 144

Optimism *by Helen Keller*   ISBN: *1-59462-108-X* **$15.95**
Helen Keller was blind, deaf, and mute since 19 months old, yet famously learned how to overcome these handicaps, communicate with the world, and spread her lectures promoting optimism. An inspiring read for everyone... Biographies/Inspirational Pages 84

Sara Crewe *by Frances Burnett*   ISBN: *1-59462-360-0* **$9.45**
In the first place, Miss Minchin lived in London. Her home was a large, dull, tall one, in a large, dull square, where all the houses were alike, and all the sparrows were alike, and where all the door-knockers made the same heavy sound... Childrens/Classic Pages 88

The Autobiography of Benjamin Franklin *by Benjamin Franklin*   ISBN: *1-59462-135-7* **$24.95**
The Autobiography of Benjamin Franklin has probably been more extensively read than any other American historical work, and no other book of its kind has had such ups and downs of fortune. Franklin lived for many years in England, where he was agent... Biographies/History Pages 332

Name	
Email	
Telephone	
Address	
City, State ZIP	

☐ **Credit Card**   ☐ **Check / Money Order**

Credit Card Number	
Expiration Date	
Signature	

Please Mail to: Book Jungle
                     PO Box 2226
                     Champaign, IL 61825
or Fax to: 630-214-0564

ORDERING INFORMATION

web*: www.bookjungle.com*
email*: sales@bookjungle.com*
fax*: 630-214-0564*
mail*: Book Jungle PO Box 2226 Champaign, IL 61825*
or PayPal *to sales@bookjungle.com*

Please contact us for bulk discounts

DIRECT-ORDER TERMS

**20% Discount if You Order
Two or More Books**
Free Domestic Shipping!
Accepted: Master Card, Visa,
Discover, American Express